Also by Lidia Matticchio Bastianich

Lidia's Family Kitchen: Nonna's Birthday Surprise
Lidia's Favorite Recipes
Lidia's Italy in America
Nonna Tell Me a Story: Lidia's Christmas Kitchen
Lidia Cooks from the Heart of Italy
Lidia's Italy
Lidia's Family Table
Lidia's Italian-American Kitchen
Lidia's Italian Table
La Cucina di Lidia

Lidia's Commonsense Italian Cooking

Lidia's Commonsense Italian Cooking

150 Delicious and Simple Recipes Anyone Can Master

Lidia Matticchio Bastianich and Tanya Bastianich Manuali

Photographs by Marcus Nilsson

Alfred A. Knopf   New York   2013

This Is a Borzoi Book
Published by Alfred A. Knopf

www.aaknopf.com

Knopf, Borzoi Books, and the colophon are registered trademarks
of Random House, Inc.

Library of Congress Cataloging-in-Publication Data
Bastianich, Lidia.
Lidia's commonsense Italian cooking : 150 delicious and simple recipes anyone
can master / by Lidia Matticchio Bastianich and Tanya Bastianich Manuali ;
photographs by Marcus Nilsson.—First edition.
pages   cm
"This is a Borzoi book"—Title page verso.
Includes index.
ISBN 978-0-385-34944-4 (alkaline paper)
1. Cooking, Italian.   I. Manuali, Tanya Bastianich.
II. Title.   III. Title: Lidia's commonsense Italian cooking.
IV. Title: Commonsense Italian cooking.
TX723.B317 2013   641.5945—dc23   2013005067

Interior photography by Marcus Nilsson
Front-of-jacket photograph © Marcus Nilsson
Jacket design by Kelly Blair
Designed by M. Kristen Bearse

Manufactured in the United States of America
First Edition

This book is dedicated to my mother, Erminia, or Nonna Mima as the family calls her. At ninety-three years of age, she still has a twinkle in her eyes and is full of love, affection, and wisdom. As my grandson Lorenzo, fourteen years old, put it in a recent speech:

> "To Nonna Mima, someone to whom seventy is young and anything over twenty dollars is expensive . . . Nonna Mima often says, *'Experientia est magistra vitae,'* meaning 'Experience is the teacher of life,' and with ninety-three years of experience she should know. . . . The life knowledge passed down to me by Nonna Mima is invaluable. She is the fundamental force that drives me to excel and enjoy life. Her story is a story of perseverance, appreciation, imparting knowledge, but most importantly, never giving up hope. . . . Nonna Mima is the root of our family system."

Common sense in an uncommon degree is
what the world calls wisdom.

—Samuel Taylor Coleridge

Common sense is not so common.

—Voltaire

Contents

Salads

Soups

Sauces

Vegetables and Sides

Pastas, Polenta, and Risottos

Fish

Meat

Desserts

The Wisdom of the Table

❀ When I think of my grandmother's kitchen, the family table is what comes to mind first. It was the wooden table with light-blue painted legs where we had our meals, where we gathered every day, ate, shared our food, our stories, and our lives. That was long ago, and now I often ask myself: Why am I a chef, and why am I so passionate about food? Why do I find peace and consolation among farmers and seasonal vegetables? Why do eggs and cheese caress my soul, and why is the crunch of crusty bread music to my ears? Why does the smell of rosemary and basil awaken my spirit? Why is the crackling skin of a roast and the mellowness of braised Swiss chard and roasted potatoes so gratifying? Why, when all the chairs are filled at a table and chatter fills the air, does my heart palpitate and my being shiver? Why have I dedicated my life to cooking for family, friends, and strangers? Why am I so gratified in doing this?

It is all about Grandma's kitchen table. That table was not in a separate room, the dining room; it was in the center of the kitchen. At that table, stories were told by the elders, and our futures were discussed and projected with wisdom. At that table, I was fed, nurtured, and loved.

I decided that I wanted never to leave that table, but to stay close to it for the rest of my life. And so I remained in the kitchen.

Today it is ever more difficult for families to gather at the dinner table, with wholesome and nutritious food to share. Business has prevailed, and the availability of fast food has changed our priorities. The seasons and the gifts they bring are not anticipated, the natural gifts of nature are altered, and friends and family are less and less likely to gather around the table for a meal.

But among the increasing interest in and discussion of recipes and food, I hear echoes. I hear a wanting, a longing, for people to reset that table. There is great wisdom in returning to the kitchen and relighting the fires that can bring families eating together, friends gathering, and people from different cultures eating one another's food, discussing their differences, and maybe even resolving world peace.

Is that too much to ask for . . . too much to hope for?

No, I do not think so; all it takes is resetting that table in the kitchen.

—Lidia

Acknowledgments

❀ I need to thank the many people who have helped me do what I love most—cook, teach, and record it all in cookbooks. In this book in particular, I share with you wisdom acquired in my many years of cooking, the importance of food, and the benefits that good cooking can provide to your life, your family, and your well-being. Wise cooking is not just about proper nutrition or delicious taste; it is just as much about what happens at the table and in our lives.

I have many people to thank for helping me collect these recipes, test them, photograph them, and, ultimately, compile it all into this book.

To Peter Gethers, Christina Malach, and Jade Noik—my Knopf dream team; their editorial skills, thoughtful advice, and extreme organization are almost all one needs to write a book. The time spent with them has been wonderful, and much more than a collaboration on this book. Thanks to my kitchen companion, Amy Stevenson, for her precise testing and recording of the recipes for this book, as well as for being our culinary producer for the companion TV series. We have spent many hot hours in the kitchen together and developed a great family friendship. Sometimes Amy brings along her children, Eli and Lily, and they love spending time with Grandma Erminia while we test recipes. After all, cooking is a family affair.

Thank you to Marcus Nilsson, friend and food photographer, whose every photo of my food induces salivation and a desire to go and cook. For tying up all the efforts and hard work into a wonderful design, thank you to Carol Carson, Kelly Blair, and Kristen Bearse. A special thanks to my dear friend Paul Bogaards for his continued enthusiasm and belief in my work, to his team for the endless efforts in marketing and promoting my works, especially to Sara Eagle.

Thanks to Robert Barnett and Deneen Howell of Williams Connelly (wc.com) for their ever-faithful and infinitely wise counsel. This book would not have happened without them.

And a great big thank-you to my mother, Erminia. Her dedication and sacrifice for me and my children cannot be measured; and as the years go by, at ninety-three, she is still always there to support us and cheer us on. Her love is an immeasurable source of strength for me. A very special heartfelt thank-you to the woman who works tirelessly alongside of me, my daughter, Tanya. She captures my enthusiasm, passion, and energy, adds her own, and simply makes things happen. Working with my daughter and her talents gives me a renewed source of inner strength, love, and "do it now" power that keeps me going. Thanks also to my son, Joe, a strong business partner and supporter. Thank you to my daughter-in-law, Deanna, for taking care of my son and my precious grandchildren. Thank you to my son-in-law, Corrado, for supporting my new business ventures with sound legal advice and good business sense. And not enough could be said about my love for my five little darlings: Olivia, Lorenzo, Miles, Ethan, and Julia. They are the source of the energy, joy, and love that fuel me. Thank you all for being the greatest family a mother could wish for.

Thank you to Shelly Burgess Nicotra, for being by my side for the past sixteen years, for her great skills at making the magic of television happen, and for managing the production of my public-television series. Thank you for your wisdom in marketing, all the while raising three beautiful children, Julia, Alex, and Luca. Planning and following Lidia on the move is not an easy task, but you do it well. *Grazie!*

As well to my office team—Lauren Falk, Cecilia Guarnaccia Trotta, Rebecca Fornaby, and Alexi Caputo—thank you for your input along the way and for holding down the fort.

In addition to those who help with my books, there are people I would like to thank for making my show on public television possible. Thank you to the American Public Television team for always doing a stellar job distributing my show. And thanks to the wonderful team at my presenting station, WGBH in Boston. Their enthusiasm is contagious, and their professionalism is exemplary. My show would not be possible without my sponsors: Cento, Il Consorzio del Grana Padano, and Monini. I thank them for believing in what I do and for their support. Thank you also to the following companies for contributing: Lidia's Pasta and Sauce, Le Creuset, OXO, Pat LaFrieda Meat Purveyors, Segafredo, Keil Brothers Nursery, Simon Pearce, The Conran Shop, Canvas Home Store, Vietri, Fairway, Cuisinart, Cornerstone Studios, D'Artagnan, Baldor Specialty Foods, and Bastianich wines.

To the many people who make sure my business continues while I am filming and writing, for their dedication and hard work, thank you: the staff of Felidia, Becco, Del Posto, Lidia's Kansas City, Lidia's Pittsburgh, and Eataly.

Introduction

❁ I love teaching, whether it is how to cook, how to enjoy, how to shop, how to set the table, how to present food, or how to prepare meals for family or friends. I am ever so grateful to have been afforded the opportunity to do so through my books, my public-television show, and my restaurants. Through the years of cooking, I have developed a keen sense of kitchen wisdom. Is this the kind of wisdom that leads to the attainment of inner balance? Well, to some extent. But it is mainly an innate understanding that gives a great sense of accomplishment and confidence when we're cooking and feeding the people we love. Cooking is something we do basically for others, and when we do it with love, with knowledge, and with a pinch of kitchen wisdom, everything is easier, everything is logical, and everything turns out better for us and our loved ones.

If you read the quotes that I used to open this book, you'll realize that for me the greatest wisdom is common sense. And common sense is an essential tool when one steps into the kitchen. I hope this book encourages you to use your common sense in cooking. My recipes are not written in stone. They are meant to be a guide. They will be better if you adapt them to your own taste (and your family's table, of course). Don't be afraid to make substitutions. Don't be afraid to add or subtract. Don't be afraid of anything when cooking. That is perhaps the greatest wisdom I can impart: never be afraid of trying or doing anything in the kitchen!

In this book, my recipes and cooking instructions are sprinkled with some simple, basic truisms. Think of them as a sprinkling of salt; we all know that sometimes a touch of salt is the one missing ingredient to set everything in balance. The recipes I chose for this book are recipes that I truly enjoy cooking and serving; they are easy to make, as well as seasonal, nutritious, and economical. These are recipes you will love cooking and serving to your family and friends, and each comes with a message. Use local fresh products, cook with the seasons, recycle rather than waste, make the time to join your family and friends at the table for a meal, do not forget to cook for yourself, and sit down and really enjoy all of the above!

Some of the recipes in this book use ingredients such as old bread (Bread and Basil Soup) or leftover lettuce (Lettuce Risotto), and I really like that: no wasting food in

my kitchen or now, I hope, in your kitchen, either. Most of the recipes in this book are quick and simple and provide easy nutrition and great flavor, such as the crunchy Carrot and Apple Salad or the Ditalini with Lentils and Shrimp. Many of the recipes give great value and nutrition and provide a full meal at lower cost. Who could resist a warm hearty bowl of Bean Soup the way it's prepared in the Le Marche region of Italy? There is so much to be said about the great value of dried beans. I love how the use of fresh and dried herbs adds so much flavor, making it easy to use less butter or oil. Vitamin-and-mineral-rich vegetables such as cauliflower, Swiss chard, and string beans are inexpensive, and increasing the vegetable-and-protein ratio in relation to your pasta makes nutritional sense. And sometimes we just need to cook from what is in our pantry, and that is when I make Oregano Eggs, Barley Soup, Garlic Risotto, or Olive Oil and Rosemary Spaghettini—all of them easy, flavorful, and delicious.

The aroma of these recipes will waft through your home and lure your family and guests to the table, and that is where you want everybody parked, because with every shared bite comes love, wisdom, and tender, loving care. Feeding ourselves, our friends, and our families is one of the most important things we do in our lives. The ingredients of great meals are fresh and have high nutritional value. They do not have to cost a lot, but they do have to be served with conviviality and love.

I always beckon people to join me at my table: "*Tutti a tavola a mangiare.*" I am sure these recipes will help you to do the same.

—Lidia

APPETIZERS

Antipasti are the foods offered before the meal itself begins. They awaken our senses and prepare us for the coming meal. The offerings are usually diversified and colorful, with lots of flavor and texture—aspects to consider when preparing an antipasto. A good antipasto stimulates and tantalizes the taste buds, like the prelude to a good symphony.

So, when preparing an antipasto, think of a colorful presentation, and if that means choosing unlikely food combinations, that is fine. You want the antipasto to instigate, to beckon people to the table. Cured products, such as prosciutto, salami, cheese, anchovies, artichokes, olives, and capers, all have developed concentrated flavors in their curing. Since the flavors of these products are intense, an antipasto made of them should be small. But when you prepare an antipasto platter, make sure it has some of those intensely flavored cured foods, like the anchovies in Anchovied Eggs (page 3) and Anchovy Frittata (page 8) or the Dijon mustard in the Mozzarella and Celery Salad (page 11), or the Seasoned Olives (page 14), which all make a great appetizer. Vegetables fit well in the appetizer mix, because they are light and diversified, but they need to have some flavor knocked into them as well, like the anchovies in the Peppers Piedmontese (page 9), or the tuna and capers in Tuna-Stuffed Artichokes (page 18).

So let your creative spirit fly when thinking of antipasti and avail yourself of a lot of cured products from your cupboard. Do not feel pressured to have an antipasto before every meal. Not every meal in Italy begins with one, and sometimes the antipasto buffet can be turned into a whole meal, as well as into sandwiches made with the leftovers the next day.

ANCHOVIED EGGS

Uova alle Acciughe

Deviled eggs have inexplicably fallen from grace on today's tables, but I think that a simple boiled egg, if dressed correctly, is delicious and contemporary. This recipe will prove my point.

Serves 4 to 6

3 tablespoons extra-virgin olive oil, plus more for drizzling

4 anchovies, chopped (about 2 tablespoons)

1 small onion, chopped

1 tablespoon fresh thyme leaves, chopped

4 small ripe plum tomatoes, seeded and chopped

¼ cup drained tiny capers in brine

½ teaspoon dried Italian oregano

2 tablespoons chopped fresh Italian parsley

8 large eggs, hard-boiled, peeled, and halved lengthwise

To a large skillet, over medium heat, add the olive oil. When the oil is hot, add the anchovies, and cook and stir until they dissolve. Add the onion, and cook until it begins to soften, about 4 minutes. Add the thyme and tomatoes, and cook until the tomatoes begin to release their juices, about 4 minutes.

Stir in the capers, oregano, and parsley, and cook until thickened, about 2 minutes.

To serve, spoon a bed of sauce onto a serving platter. Arrange eggs, cut side up, on the platter, and spoon the rest of the sauce over the eggs.

OREGANO EGGS

Uova all'Origano

This is one of the simplest and yet tastiest preparations of eggs I've ever had. One afternoon, a friend and I unexpectedly dropped in on my friend Mario in Trieste. It was lunchtime, and he had a big basket full of fresh eggs he had brought down from the Carso, the high plateau surrounding Trieste. Eggs it was for lunch, served with a bowl of radicchio salad. We were just a few people that day, but this recipe is so very easy to modify for smaller or larger groups.

Serves 4

2 tablespoons extra-virgin olive oil

8 large eggs

¼ teaspoon kosher salt

½ teaspoon dried oregano

¼ cup grated Grana Padano or Parmigiano-Reggiano

QUICK TIP

It can be difficult to crack eggs into a skillet for frying. Instead, you can crack two eggs into a small glass bowl and then slide them into the skillet when it's hot.

Set a large (12-inch) nonstick skillet over a burner that's still off. Swirl the pan with the olive oil, and gently break all the eggs to fill the pan, taking care not to break the yolks. Sprinkle with the salt and dried oregano. Sprinkle the grated cheese over all.

Cover the skillet, and turn the flame to medium-low. Cook until the whites are set and the yolks are done to your liking, about 7 to 8 minutes for still-runny yolks.

This is a great breakfast or main course, or, served over some arugula, it can be an appetizer.

Facing page, top: Genovese Focaccia (page 32); bottom: Oregano Eggs

I love eggs. They are economical, a great source of nutrients, and easy to prepare. In the past decade, eggs came under attack for their high cholesterol content, but that has rightfully and fortunately subsided now—eggs are back in vogue. When I was growing up in Italy, eggs were used as the main source of protein for many a meal. They were boiled as an addition to salads, whisked into broths with vegetables, made into frittatas with all kinds of vegetables and small amounts of meat added, or just simply scrambled or poached all by themselves.

Of utmost importance is that the egg be fresh and that it come from an organic or free-range chicken. To test the freshness of an egg, crack it and set it on a flat plate. Notice if the ring of albumen, the white part around the yolk, is thick and forms a circle around the yolk. If it does, then the egg is fresh. If the albumen is watery and runny and spreads all over the plate, it is most likely still good to eat but less fresh—and thus less tasty.

When baking with eggs, it is always best to have the eggs at room temperature before cracking.

ANCHOVY FRITTATA

Frittata di Acciughe

This frittata could be a great lunch, but the salty, savory anchovies make it a great appetizer, sliced or cubed. Served with some dressed arugula, it is delightful. Any leftovers make a great sandwich the next day.

Serves 6

12 large eggs

½ cup whole milk

1 teaspoon kosher salt

½ cup grated Grana Padano or Parmigiano-Reggiano

2 cups crustless day-old bread cubes, from a loaf of country bread

¼ cup extra-virgin olive oil

1 pound medium zucchini, thinly sliced

1 small onion, thinly sliced

1 bunch scallions, trimmed and chopped

12 good-quality anchovy fillets

Preheat the oven to 400 degrees F. In a large bowl, beat the eggs with the milk, salt, and cheese. Stir in the bread cubes, and let the bread soak while you cook the zucchini.

In a 12-inch nonstick skillet, over medium heat, heat the olive oil. When it is hot, add the zucchini, onion, and scallions. Cook until softened, about 5 minutes.

Spread the vegetables out to cover the bottom of the skillet, and pour the eggs and bread over them. Arrange the anchovies on top like spokes in a wheel.

Set the skillet with the frittata in the oven, and bake until the top is golden and the eggs are set, about 20 to 25 minutes. Slide a paring knife around the edge of the skillet to help unmold if the frittata seems to be sticking. Slide onto a cutting board, cut into slices, and serve.

PEPPERS PIEDMONTESE

Peperoni alla Piemontese

Just about everybody is familiar with fried peppers, but try adding a fillet or two of anchovies, as they do in Piemonte, and the flavor path takes another superb twist. Just be attentive with the salt, since the anchovies deliver a good dose of it. This dish is a great addition to any antipasto or buffet table, and delicious when added to a bun with a juicy burger.

Serves 6

6 yellow or red bell peppers

3 tablespoons extra-virgin olive oil

6 garlic cloves, peeled and sliced

8 anchovies, chopped

¼ teaspoon kosher salt

3 tablespoons chopped fresh Italian parsley

Char the peppers as they are—whole and uncleaned—on the stove flame on all sides (or under the broiler). Immediately put the charred peppers in a large bowl and cover tightly with plastic wrap. Let them steam until cool. Peel the charred skin from peppers, remove the stems and seeds, and cut into 1-inch-thick strips.

To a large skillet, over medium heat, add the olive oil. When the oil is hot, add the garlic. Once the garlic begins to sizzle, add the anchovies. Sauté until the anchovies fall apart and dissolve into the oil. Stir together the garlic, anchovies, and grilled pepper strips, and season with the salt. Sprinkle with some parsley, and toss 3 to 4 minutes, so the peppers absorb the garlic-and-anchovy flavor. Serve peppers warm or at room temperature.

Mozzarella is best when it was made the same day and has not yet been in the refrigerator. In Campania, the region of which Naples is the capital, where mozzarella is king, they deem it best within 3 hours after it has been made. Mozzarella—*fior di latte,* as it is called in Italy—is made from the freshest whole cow's milk. It is milky and rich in taste and at the same time has a resilient texture. There should be a milky juiciness in every bite. Fresh mozzarella should not be runny or acidic. Mozzarella can also be made from the milk of the water buffalo, and appropriately called *mozzarella di bufala.* Keep mozzarella packaged in the refrigerator until ready to use, but let it stand at room temperature 15 minutes before eating it.

MOZZARELLA AND CELERY SALAD

Insalata di Mozzarella e Sedano

Everybody is familiar with the Caprese salad, the perfect combination of tomato and mozzarella, or mozzarella and roasted peppers. This recipe made with celery instead is a fresh and tasty alternative, especially in the winter months, when tomatoes are not at their best.

Serves 6

2 tablespoons fresh lemon juice

2 teaspoons Dijon mustard

¼ teaspoon kosher salt

3 tablespoons extra-virgin olive oil

1 pound fresh mozzarella, cubed

½ cup walnuts, toasted and coarsely chopped

2 cups celery thinly sliced on the bias, with some leaves

In a serving bowl, whisk together the lemon juice, mustard, and salt. Then slowly whisk in the olive oil to make a smooth dressing.

Add the mozzarella, walnuts, and celery. Toss well with the dressing, and serve. Or you can plate a more formal version with fanned, sliced mozzarella and the dressed celery and walnuts on top.

RAW GARDEN SALAD

Giardiniera sott'Olio

This is a very appealing way to prepare and present vegetables in the summer, when produce is abundant; it stays crisp and crunchy in the refrigerator for quite a while. I use these pickled vegetables on a buffet table as a side dish with grilled meats, or toss them into a salad. They also work wonderfully well topped with canned tuna or a sliced chicken breast, and they make a great addition to a sandwich. As you use the giardiniera vegetables, make sure you also use the oil they are packed in.

Serves 6

2 cups carrot sticks 1½ inches long

2 cups haricots verts, trimmed

2 cups small cauliflower florets

1 cup sliced red onion

⅓ cup coarse sea salt

3 cups white-wine vinegar

2 cups extra-virgin olive oil, or more as needed

In a large nonreactive bowl, toss the vegetables with the salt. Cover, and refrigerate overnight.

Rinse both the vegetables and the bowl well, and return the vegetables to the bowl. Toss with the vinegar. Cover, and refrigerate for 4 hours or up to overnight.

Rinse and drain again. Pack the vegetables snugly into a lidded glass jar (a quart-sized jar works perfectly). Pour in the olive oil to cover the vegetables. Close the lid, and refrigerate until ready to serve. To serve, fish out the vegetables needed and drizzle some of the curing oil on top. Save the oil to dress other salads.

SEASONED OLIVES

Olive alla Marchigiana

The selection of olives one can buy today is extraordinary. In a good food market one can find thirty varietals or more to buy. Olives are as loved and sought after today as they have been through the centuries. They are nutritionally sound and bring strong flavor and texture to our table and whatever we are cooking. So, when you cannot find that flavored olive you yearn for, make your own. Here is a simple recipe that I am sure will gratify you and your guests.

Serves 6 to 8

1 pound brine-cured black olives with pits

1 large orange, zest removed with a peeler and julienned, orange juiced

3 garlic cloves, peeled and crushed

½ teaspoon ground fennel

Pinch crushed red-pepper flakes

2 tablespoons extra-virgin olive oil

In a large bowl, toss together the olives, orange zest and juice, garlic, fennel, red-pepper flakes, and olive oil. Pack the mixture into a glass jar, and let the olives marinate for 3 to 4 days in the refrigerator. Remove the garlic, and serve. Olives will keep for several weeks in the refrigerator.

QUICK TIP

To grind fennel seeds, just pulse them in a spice grinder.

CHICKEN BREAST SALAD
Insalata di Pollo

Classic chicken salad is an American favorite, and it makes excellent sandwiches, but in today's reality, when we are all looking for healthier, more sensible dishes for our families, this recipe is a solid option. It is delicious, first and foremost, easy to prepare, and a great recipe to use to recycle roasted or rotisserie chicken that you might have in your refrigerator.

Serves 6

2½ pounds bone-in, skin-on chicken breasts

1 medium carrot, peeled and cut into chunks

1 celery stalk, cut into chunks (about 1 cup), plus 3 stalks, leaves plucked, thinly sliced

1 medium onion, cut into chunks

Handful fresh parsley sprigs

3 tablespoons Dijon mustard

4 anchovy fillets

Juice of 2 lemons

¼ teaspoon kosher salt

¼ cup extra-virgin olive oil

⅓ cup drained tiny capers in brine

3 ripe medium tomatoes, cut into 12 slices

Put the chicken, the chunks of carrot, celery, and onion, and the parsley in a pot with cold water to cover by a few inches. Bring to a simmer, and simmer gently until the chicken is cooked through, about 15 to 20 minutes. Let the chicken cool in the cooking liquid. Remove the chicken, discard the skin and bones, and shred the meat into a large bowl. (Don't throw away the cooking liquid—save it for a soup or risotto!)

In a mini–food processor, combine the mustard, anchovies, lemon juice, and salt. With the machine running, drizzle in the olive oil to make a smooth, creamy dressing. Drizzle the dressing over the chicken, add the sliced celery stalk and leaves, and capers, and toss to coat. Arrange the tomato slices on a platter, season with salt, and mound the chicken salad on the tomatoes.

BOILED BEEF SALAD WITH GHERKINS, RED ONION, AND PARSLEY

Insalata di Manzo Bollito con Cetrioli, Cipolla Rossa, e Prezzemolo

I love boiled beef. In the northern regions of Italy, it is the basis of a common dish called bollito misto, *in which there is capon, tongue, veal head, cotechino (a great pork head sausage), and beef. Making a* bollito misto *is a complicated procedure, but making this delicious boiled-beef salad is not. You boil the beef, which, in the process, gives you a great pot of stock as well. The poaching liquid for the beef can be strained and served as a soup with some pastina and grated Grana Padano or Parmigiano-Reggiano cheese.*

Serves 6 to 8

4 carrots, peeled and cut into large chunks or thick slices

1 onion, cut into large chunks

3 celery stalks, cut into large chunks

3 tablespoons chopped fresh Italian parsley leaves (reserve stems)

2-pound piece boneless beef top chuck

¾ teaspoon kosher salt

1 cup halved cornichons

½ medium red onion, thinly sliced

3 tablespoons red-wine vinegar

1 tablespoon Dijon mustard

¼ cup extra-virgin olive oil

In a large soup pot, combine 8 quarts cold water, the carrots, onion, celery, reserved parsley stems, and beef. Bring to a simmer, and simmer until the beef is very tender, about 1½ hours. Let cool, and pull out the beef and carrots (strain the stock for another use). Chop the carrots, and put in a serving bowl. Dice the beef, add it to the bowl, and season all with ½ teaspoon of the salt.

Add the cornichons and red onion. In a small bowl, whisk together the vinegar, mustard, and remaining ¼ teaspoon salt. Whisk in the olive oil to make a smooth, creamy dressing. Drizzle the dressing over the beef salad, and add the parsley leaves. Toss well and serve.

TUNA-STUFFED ARTICHOKES

Carciofi Ripieni di Tonno

Are stuffed artichokes worth all the effort in the preparation? An Italian would say, "Yes, of course!" They are a delicacy, especially in the springtime and early summer. Stuffed with bread-crumbs and seasoning, they make a classic dish. When tuna is added, the dish becomes more substantial and deliciously different. This is a great appetizer.

Serves 6 as appetizer

2 lemons, 1 zested, both juiced

6 large artichokes

Two 5-ounce cans Italian tuna in oil, drained

1 cup dried breadcrumbs

¼ cup drained tiny capers in brine

2 hard-boiled eggs, peeled and finely chopped

¼ cup chopped fresh Italian parsley

½ cup extra-virgin olive oil

1 cup white wine

¼ teaspoon crushed red-pepper flakes

½ teaspoon kosher salt

QUICK TIP

You can save the juiced shells of lemons by freezing them, and then use them when you need acidulated water.

Preheat the oven to 375 degrees F. Fill a bowl with cold water, and add the juice of one lemon, plus the squeezed-out lemon halves. To clean artichokes for stuffing, trim the stems so the artichokes will sit up straight, peel the stems, and pull off any tough outer leaves from the artichokes and discard. Using a paring knife, trim away any tough parts around the base and stem of the artichoke. With a serrated knife, cut off the top third of the artichoke and discard. Push the leaves out to expose the fuzzy purple choke. With a small spoon, scrape out the choke to expose the heart at the bottom of the artichoke. Put the prepared artichoke in the bowl of water.

For the stuffing: In a medium bowl, break up the tuna with a fork. Stir in the breadcrumbs, lemon zest (grated), capers, chopped eggs, 3 tablespoons of the parsley, and ¼ cup of the olive oil.

Drain the artichokes, and spoon the stuffing into the center, between the leaves of the artichokes. Use your fingers to pry the leaves open. Fit the stuffed artichokes into a 9-by-13-inch baking dish (or any size that will fit them snugly). In a spouted measuring cup, whisk together the wine, juice of the other lemon, 3 tablespoons of olive oil, the red-pepper flakes, salt, and remaining 1 tablespoon parsley. Pour the sauce around the artichokes in the baking dish. Drizzle the artichokes with remaining tablespoon olive oil. Cover with foil, and bake until artichokes are tender throughout, about 40 minutes. Uncover, and bake until the stuffing is browned and crisp, about 20 minutes. Serve warm or at room temperature.

CLAM BRUSCHETTA

Bruschetta alle Vongole

Pasta dressed with clam sauce has been a favorite in Italian households and Italian restaurants since forever, but have you ever tried to drown a piece of crusty Italian bread, still warm from the grill, with clam sauce? Well, here it is, and I promise this will become a favorite bruschetta in your home. It makes a delicious hors d'oeuvre, but it can also make a meal. It is a very good addition to a grilling party: have a bowl of this sauce handy, and as the bread comes off the grill, let everyone douse it with a spoonful of the sauce.

Serves 6

¼ cup extra-virgin olive oil

1 large onion, thinly sliced (about 1½ cups)

4 garlic cloves, peeled and thinly sliced

Pinch crushed red-pepper flakes

½ teaspoon kosher salt

48 littleneck clams, shucked, shucking juices reserved and strained (about 1 cup meat, 1½ cups shucking juices), clams chopped if they are large

¼ cup chopped fresh Italian parsley

12 thick slices country bread, each 2 to 3 inches long, grilled

To a large skillet, over medium-high heat, add the olive oil. When the oil is hot, add the onion. Cook, stirring occasionally, until the onion is softened, about 4 minutes. Add the garlic, and let sizzle a minute, taking care not to burn it, then season with the crushed red-pepper flakes and salt.

Add the clam-shucking juices to the skillet, bring to a boil, and add the parsley. Let boil to reduce the juices by about half and bring the sauce together. Reduce the heat to a simmer, add the shucked clams, and simmer until they are just cooked, about 2 minutes.

Divide the sauce evenly over the grilled bread, and serve hot.

TOMATO AND RICOTTA CROSTINI

Crostini alla Ricotta e Pomodori

Crostini and bruschette are part of everybody's vocabulary and table, and these crostini are tasty and easy to make. The good part is that you can prepare them all in advance and just pop them in the oven when your guests arrive. When making this crostini, or for that matter any crostini or bruschetta, try using whole-grain or whole-wheat bread. My grandmother always used a multigrain bread that contained some bran. So, if you are thinking Italian, think rustic and healthy.

Serves 6

6 tablespoons extra-virgin olive oil

6 large, thick slices of Italian-style whole-wheat bread

4 ripe medium tomatoes, diced (about 2 cups)

½ cup pitted green olives, sliced

¼ loosely packed cup fresh basil leaves, coarsely shredded

½ teaspoon kosher salt

1 cup drained fresh ricotta

Preheat oven to 375 degrees F. Brush the bread with 3 tablespoons olive oil, and place on a rimmed baking sheet. In a medium bowl, toss together the tomatoes, olives, basil, and salt. Drizzle with the remaining 3 tablespoons olive oil, and toss.

Mound the tomato mixture evenly on each of the bread slices on the baking sheet, and top each with ricotta. Bake until the bread is toasted and the topping is warmed through, about 10 to 15 minutes. Serve hot.

BAKED COUNTRY VEGETABLES

Tortino Campagnolo

Think of this dish as vegetable lasagna, luscious seasonal vegetables layered with tomato sauce and cheese, then baked until bubbly and delicious. It could be a main course, a side dish, or an appetizer. The leftovers reheat beautifully and can be used as filling for a sandwich. This dish also keeps well in the freezer. Once it is cold, cut one-portion squares, wrap, label (and date) it, and freeze it. To reheat, bring to room temperature, and reheat in the oven or toaster oven.

Serves 6

1 pound medium eggplant, thinly sliced lengthwise

½ teaspoon kosher salt, plus more for salting the eggplant

Vegetable oil, for frying the vegetables

All-purpose flour, for dredging

1 pound medium zucchini, thinly sliced lengthwise

1 tablespoon softened unsalted butter, for the baking dish

8 ounces low-moisture mozzarella, shredded

1 cup grated Grana Padano or Parmigiano-Reggiano

1½ cups Marinara Sauce (page 80)

Season the eggplant slices liberally with salt. Fan out in a large colander. Set a large bowl inside, weighted with cans, to help press the excess liquid and bitterness from the eggplant. After about 20 minutes, rinse and drain the eggplant, and pat dry.

Preheat oven to 400 degrees F. In a large skillet, heat about ¼ inch of vegetable oil over medium-high heat. When the oil is hot but not smoking, dredge the eggplant in flour, tapping off the excess, and fry in batches until browned and crisp on both sides, about 2 minutes per side. Drain on paper towels. Season the zucchini with the ½ teaspoon salt, and dredge in flour. Fry until browned and crisp on both sides, about 2 minutes per side. Drain with the eggplant.

Grease an 8-by-8-inch ceramic or glass baking dish with the butter. In a bowl, toss together the mozzarella and Grana Padano. Spread ½ cup of the marinara sauce in the bottom of the dish. Fan out a layer of half the vegetables, like shingles. Sprinkle with half of the cheese. Spread another ½ cup of the sauce. Fan the remaining vegetables out, then cover with the remaining sauce, and sprinkle the top with the remaining cheese. Bake, uncovered, until bubbly and the cheese is browned and crusty, about 30 minutes.

In Italy, there are many delicious recipes that involve making a crust. Vegetables baked in a crust, bound by some eggs and flavored with cheese and herbs, make a meal that can be eaten hot out of the oven, at room temperature, or reheated the next day and be just as good in each incarnation. These crusted recipes freeze very well, so you can divide them into four parts and freeze them for future use. Make sure you wrap them well; to reheat, pop them in the microwave, or, if you like them even crisper, let them defrost, then set them in the toaster oven to crisp up.

RUSTIC RICOTTA TART

Torta Rustica di Ricotta

In the Italian cuisine, dough is at the center of many dishes, whether turned into pasta, crostata, pizza, or torta. The dough is the carrier of other delicious products, be they vegetables, meats, fish, or cheeses. In Italian tortas, ricotta is one of the favorite fillers, often with eggs to bind it. One can flavor ricotta with just about anything; in this dish I use ham and mozzarella. Just think of all the other meats and vegetables you can add to give this recipe your family's special flavor twist.

Serves 6 to 8

1 tablespoon unsalted butter, at room temperature

All-purpose flour, for rolling

1 sheet frozen puff pastry, thawed

1 pound (2 cups) fresh ricotta, drained

4 large eggs, beaten

1 cup cubed low-moisture mozzarella

1 cup julienned strips deli ham

⅓ cup grated Grana Padano or Parmigiano-Reggiano

Preheat the oven to 375 degrees F. Grease a 10-by-7-inch baking dish with the butter. Roll out the puff pastry on a lightly floured surface into a rectangle about 14 by 11 inches. Fit the dough into the prepared baking dish, letting the dough go up and extend over the sides.

In a large bowl, mix together the ricotta, three eggs, the mozzarella, ham, and grated cheese to combine. Spread filling over the dough, and fold the dough over to make a 1- or 2-inch border. Press holes in the top dough with a fork, and brush it with the remaining egg. Bake until the filling is set and the pastry is golden and crisp, about 40 minutes. Let the tart rest on a rack for at least 15 minutes, to set, before cutting into squares and serving.

RICOTTA AND VEGETABLE CROSTATA
Crostata di Ricotta e Verdure

This is a great recipe your friends and family will love. You can easily make it your own by changing the flavoring agents. You can omit the anchovies and change the vegetable. Just make sure, when braising the vegetable, that it is cooked dry. If the vegetable has released a lot of water—such as squash would, for example—then drain it before adding it to the ricotta.

Serves 6 to 8

DOUGH

2 cups all-purpose flour, plus more for rolling the dough

1 teaspoon kosher salt

½ cup extra-virgin olive oil

⅔ cup cold water

FILLING

2 tablespoons extra-virgin olive oil

2 cups chopped onions

4 anchovy fillets, chopped

3 pounds Swiss chard, washed, trimmed, leaves and stems finely chopped

2 cups drained fresh ricotta

3 large eggs, beaten, plus 1 yolk, for brushing the crust

1 cup grated Grana Padano or Parmigiano-Reggiano

½ cup heavy cream

For the dough: Pulse the flour with the salt in a food processor. In a measuring cup, mix together the oil and water. With the processor running, pour the liquid in, and process to knead into a smooth dough. Scrape dough onto the counter, knead a few times by hand, and wrap in plastic wrap. Let the dough rest at room temperature for about 30 minutes while you make the filling.

Preheat the oven to 375 degrees F. In a Dutch oven, heat the 2 tablespoons olive oil over medium heat. Add the onions, and cook until they begin to soften, about 5 minutes. Add the anchovies; cook and stir until they dissolve into the oil, about 2 minutes. Add the Swiss chard, cover, and cook until the leaves are completely tender, about 30 minutes (check occasionally to make sure the mixture is not burning). Uncover, and cook away any excess liquid, about 10 minutes. Scrape onto a sheet pan and cool.

When the chard has cooled, mix it in a large bowl with the ricotta, the three eggs, grated cheese, and cream.

On a floured surface, roll the dough to fit an oiled half sheet pan, leaving a 2-inch excess border; trim the dough to fit if necessary. Poke holes in the bottom dough with a fork. Spread the filling on the dough, fold the excess crust over to form a border that covers some of the filling, and make holes with a fork in the top dough. Beat the egg yolk with a pinch of salt, and brush the dough with the yolk. Bake until crust is browned and filling is browned on top and set throughout, about 40 minutes. Allow the tart to cool on a rack at least 10 minutes, to set, before cutting into squares and serving.

SQUASH AND RICOTTA TART

Tortino di Ricotta e Zucca

I like to use butternut squash for this recipe, but any nice meaty squash in season will do, as will a sweet potato. This is a great holiday treat, as an appetizer or as a side dish. It is like baking a cheesecake or pie: once you have done the assembling, it is basically done; just bake it and serve it warm.

Serves 6

1 pound butternut squash grated on the coarse holes of a box grater

1 cup milk

2 tablespoons sugar

3 tablespoons unsalted butter, at room temperature

¼ cup dried breadcrumbs

2 large eggs

1½ pounds fresh ricotta, drained

1 cup grated Grana Padano or Parmigiano-Reggiano

2 tablespoons chopped fresh mint

1 teaspoon kosher salt

¼ teaspoon freshly grated nutmeg

Preheat the oven to 350 degrees F. Put the squash in a medium saucepan with the milk and sugar. Simmer until the squash is tender, about 15 minutes. Let it cool, then wrap the squash in a kitchen towel, and wring out any excess water. Grease a 9-inch glass pie plate with 1 tablespoon of the butter. Sprinkle with 2 tablespoons of the breadcrumbs, and tap around to line the pie plate with the crumbs, tapping out any excess.

In a large bowl, whisk together the eggs and ricotta. Stir in the grated cheese, mint, salt, and nutmeg. Add the squash, breaking up any lumps with your fingers, and stir to incorporate into the ricotta mixture.

Spread the mixture into the pie plate, and smooth the top with a spatula. Cut the remaining butter into small pieces, and scatter on top. Sprinkle with the remaining breadcrumbs, and bake until set, about 40 to 45 minutes. Allow the tart to cool and set on a rack for at least ½ hour before cutting into wedges to serve. Serve warm or at room temperature.

ONION TART
Crostata di Cipolle

Think of pie dough when you make this dough. Do not work the dough much; you need to combine the ingredients quickly. The assembly is fast and easy. Keep the dough chilled until ready to roll it out for the tart. The rest could not be any simpler, and once it's finished you have an exquisite tart for your antipasto. I love to serve it warm with some tossed greens next to it. It's a great lunch as well.

Serves 6 to 8

DOUGH

3 cups all-purpose flour, plus more for rolling

1½ teaspoons kosher salt

2 sticks cold butter, cut into cubes

6 tablespoons cold water, plus more as needed

ONIONS

4 tablespoons butter, plus more for the cookie sheet

3 pounds onions, halved and thinly sliced

2 teaspoons kosher salt

1 cup heavy cream

½ cup grated Grana Padano or Parmigiano-Reggiano

For the dough: Pulse together the flour and salt in a food processor. Scatter in the butter cubes, and process in pulses until the butter looks like coarse crumbs. Drizzle in the water, and pulse until the dough just comes together, about 10 seconds. Add a little more water if it's too dry, or a little more flour if it's too wet. Dump the dough on a floured counter and knead a few times, until it comes together; it shouldn't be too sticky or crumbly. Wrap the dough in plastic wrap, and let it rest in the refrigerator while you prepare the onions.

Preheat oven to 350 degrees F. In a large skillet, melt the butter over medium heat. Add the onions, and season with the salt. Cook until wilted but not colored, about 10 to 15 minutes. Add the cream, bring to a simmer, and cook, covered, until tender, about 20 minutes. Uncover, and increase the heat to simmer away any excess liquid, which will take about 15 minutes. Let cool while you roll out the dough.

Butter a 15-by-10-inch rimmed cookie sheet. On a floured surface, roll out the dough to a rectangle a little larger than the cookie sheet. (If you have a hard time rolling out such a large piece of dough, roll between layers of parchment paper.) Fit the dough into the prepared pan, letting the excess dough hang over the edges. Spread the onions on the dough, and sprinkle with the grated cheese. Fold the hanging dough back over the onion to form a border crust around the edges.

Bake until crust is crisp and golden, about 40 to 45 minutes. Let cool on a rack at least 15 minutes before cutting into squares to serve.

BAKED TOAST SANDWICHES

Fagottini al Forno

This is an Italian version of a grilled cheese sandwich. The beauty of this recipe is that once you have made it you will find a hundred ways to reinvent it. Do not forget to be innovative with the bread as well: whole-wheat, mixed-grain, and muffins all work beautifully.

Serves 4

3 tablespoons unsalted butter

8 slices sturdy whole-wheat bread

8 slices low-moisture mozzarella

8 slices deli ham

¼ cup prepared tomato sauce

8 fresh basil leaves

2 tablespoons grated Grana Padano
   or Parmigiano-Reggiano

Preheat the oven to 400 degrees F. Grease a 9-by-13-inch baking dish with 1 tablespoon of the butter. Arrange four slices of the bread in the dish, not touching. Top each with one slice of cheese and two slices of the ham. Spread the tomato sauce over the ham, and top with the basil leaves, then the remaining slices of cheese. Spread the last four slices of bread with the remaining 2 tablespoons butter, and set on top of the sandwiches, butter side up. Sprinkle the bread with the grated cheese.

Bake until the bread is toasted and the cheese is melted and bubbly, about 15 minutes. Let sit for a few minutes before serving.

POTATO PIZZA
Pizza di Patate

Everybody loves pizza, but sometimes it is intimidating and seems difficult to make at home. This is a version of baked dough, but as its base it has potatoes and it is not leavened, so it's easier to handle and yet has all the flavors and feel of pizza. There are endless ways of making and baking dough in the Italian tradition, not to mention in all the different cultures of the world, but there is something basic and sacred about the simplicity of turning grains into bread. It is a direct link between the earth and sustenance for human beings. We need to reflect and understand and get to know the earth, and the food it provides. Children, especially today, are far removed from the basic source of food, so bring your children into the kitchen with you and let them feel the dough in their hands. Let them wonder how this magic can happen from the earth we stomp on.

Serves 4 to 6

1 pound russet potatoes

1½ cups all-purpose flour, plus more for rolling the dough

2 teaspoons baking powder

2½ teaspoons kosher salt

1 large egg, beaten

2 tablespoons extra-virgin olive oil, plus more for cookie sheet

12 ounces fresh mozzarella, thinly sliced

4 cherry or other small tomatoes, thinly sliced

1 teaspoon dried oregano

¼ cup grated Grana Padano or Parmigiano-Reggiano

Preheat the oven to 350 degrees F. Put the whole, unpeeled potatoes in a pot with water to cover by a couple of inches, and bring to a simmer. Cook the potatoes until they are easily pierced with a knife but not falling apart, about 20 minutes. Let them cool slightly, then peel, press through a ricer onto a sheet pan, and let cool completely.

Scrape the potatoes into a bowl, and sift over them the flour, baking powder, and salt. Mix in the egg to make a smooth dough. Oil a 15-by-10-inch cookie sheet with olive oil. On a floured surface, roll the dough out to a rectangle almost as large as the cookie sheet, or as large as you can get it. (If the dough is difficult to roll, roll between layers of parchment paper.) Transfer to the cookie sheet, and press the dough out to almost reach the edges of the pan.

Top the dough evenly with the mozzarella, leaving a ½-inch border around the edges. Top with the sliced tomatoes, then drizzle with the 2 tablespoons olive oil. Sprinkle with the dried oregano and grated cheese. Bake until the crust is browned on the bottom and cooked through, about 35 minutes. Allow the pizza to cool on the baking sheet for a few minutes before cutting into squares to serve.

GENOVESE FOCACCIA

Focaccia Genovese

Every region of Italy makes some form of focaccia, but if we want to nitpick, it seems that focaccia had its start in the Ligurian culinary tradition. In Genova, the capital city of Liguria, freshly baked focaccia studded with basil leaves enhances almost every table. But as you travel to the different regions of Italy, the herbs and flavorings will change from rosemary to oregano to olives, onion, and tomatoes. The variety of toppings on the Italian focaccia is endless. You should feel free to change this recipe by using the herb that you have in your refrigerator, or your family's favorite.

Serves 8

FOR THE FOCACCIA

1 packet active dry yeast (2 ¼ teaspoons)

1 teaspoon sugar

6 tablespoons extra-virgin olive oil

6 cups all-purpose flour, plus more
   for working the dough

2 teaspoons kosher salt

FOR THE TOPPING

3 tablespoons extra-virgin olive oil

½ cup coarsely chopped fresh basil

3 tablespoons grated Grana Padano
   or Parmigiano-Reggiano

Dissolve the yeast and sugar in ½ cup warm water (90 to 110 degrees F). Let the mixture sit a few minutes, until the yeast is bubbly.

Put the proofed yeast in a mixer fitted with the dough hook attachment. Pour in another 1½ cups warm water and 2 tablespoons olive oil. Add the flour, holding back about ½ cup of the total measured amount. Add the salt. Mix on low speed to combine into a wet dough. If the dough is still dry or seems tight, add up to ½ cup more warm water, a little at a time. If it seems too wet, add up to the remaining ½ cup flour, a little at a time. Knead the dough on medium speed until it is soft and springy and leaves the sides of the bowl clean, about 3 to 4 minutes. Dump the dough on a floured counter, and knead a few times by hand to bring together into a ball. Oil a large bowl, and toss the dough to coat. Cover, and let rise until doubled in size, about 1 to 1½ hours, depending on the temperature of your room.

Punch down the dough. Oil a half sheet pan with olive oil, and dump the dough into the sheet pan. Press with your fingers to fit dough to the edges of the pan. Let rise another 30 minutes, uncovered. Preheat oven to 400 degrees F. Once the dough has risen, gently press indentations in the dough with your fingertips, about 1 inch apart. Bake until set, about 10 to 15 minutes, pull out of oven, and brush with 1 tablespoon olive oil. Finish baking until the focaccia is golden brown on the top and bottom, about 25 minutes in all.

While the dough finishes baking, in a bowl stir together the basil, grated cheese, and the remaining olive oil. As soon as you remove focaccia from oven, spread with the basil mixture.

OATMEAL BISCUITS

Tortino d'Avena

Biscuits are not traditional in Italy, but I love them and they are easy to make. Here I make biscuits very Italian by adding chopped basil and grated cheese. Make sure you double the recipe if you have a tableful of guests—they will disappear quickly served alongside your Mozzarella and Celery Salad (page 11) or Peppers Piedmontese (page 9) or with any soup.

Makes 16 small biscuits/cakes

½ cup rolled oats (not instant)

1¾ cups all-purpose flour, plus more for kneading

1 teaspoon baking powder

½ teaspoon baking soda

½ teaspoon kosher salt

¼ cup chopped fresh basil

¼ cup grated Grana Padano or Parmigiano-Reggiano

4 tablespoons cold unsalted butter, cut into bits

¾ cup buttermilk, chilled

Preheat the oven to 425 degrees F. Line a baking sheet with parchment paper.

In a food processor, combine the oats, flour, baking powder, baking soda, and salt. Pulse once or twice, just to combine. Sprinkle in the basil and grated cheese, and pulse once to combine. Add the butter, and pulse until the mixture looks like coarse meal. Pour in the buttermilk, and pulse just until it comes together in a rough dough. Knead the dough on the counter once or twice to bring it together.

Form and press the dough into an 8-inch square on the parchment-lined baking sheet. Cut into sixteen square biscuits.

Bake until golden, about 10 to 12 minutes. Allow the biscuits to cool a bit on the baking sheet on a rack before removing them from the sheet. Serve hot or warm.

SALADS

Dress Your Salad with Wisdom

Drain your salad well before dressing it, and pass it through a spinner; otherwise, the dressing will be diluted by the remaining water and slide off the salad leaves. Once the salad has been washed and drained, let it chill in the refrigerator for an hour or two; it will get crispier.

Dress your salad as close to the serving time as possible.

Do not *over*dress your salad or it will become heavy and soggy. If you're not sure of the right amount, go light and taste it. Repeat until you're satisfied.

Choose your dressing according to the texture of the salad. If the salad is silky and tender, use a light, liquid dressing. If the salad is resilient, then the creamy and chunkier dressings are fine.

If you are using olive oil and wine vinegar, the ratio is usually a third vinegar to two-thirds olive oil. Whisk the oil and vinegar first, add some salt, and then dress the salad. To add some garlic flavor, add a few cloves of crushed garlic to the oil-and-vinegar mixture. Let it steep for 15 minutes, remove the garlic, and toss the salad with the flavored dressing. Sometimes I like to replace the vinegar with fresh lemon juice. If you like a creamier dressing, whisk a hard-boiled egg yolk into the dressing. For a little zest, add a spoonful or two of mustard or grated horseradish to the dressing.

Yogurt and sour cream are great additions to an olive-oil-and-lemon dressing. I especially like this combination to dress salads with grains and legumes.

Always add grated cheese to the salad, if called for, *after* you have dressed the salad; cheese clumps will form if you pour the dressing over salad to which cheese has been added.

TOMATO AND MINT SALAD

Insalata di Pomodori e Menta

You are most likely accustomed to the tomato-and-basil combination, but try this refreshing tomato-and-mint salad, a new twist to an old classic.

Serves 6

¼ cup loosely packed fresh mint leaves

2 pounds ripe tomatoes, cored, cut into 1-inch wedges

1 cup thinly sliced red onion

3 tablespoons extra-virgin olive oil

2 tablespoons red-wine vinegar

½ teaspoon kosher salt

Freshly ground black pepper, to taste

Shred the mint. Put the tomatoes in a salad bowl with the onion and mint. Toss with the olive oil and vinegar. Season with salt and pepper.

How to Choose Tomatoes for Salad

Tomatoes are a delicious and versatile vegetable, rich in vitamin C and lycopene. Even better, just about everyone loves tomatoes. So how do you choose tomatoes for a salad? Look for tomatoes that are grown locally, the closer the better. If not local, tomatoes are often picked green and ripened off the vine, producing fruit that has not properly or fully developed its flavor. The best tomatoes are in season, and usually the farmers' markets carry these. I also look for tomatoes that have stems attached, which allow them to retain their flavor and stay fresh. The stem and leaves of the tomato should be green and tightly attached. Brownish, loose leaves or stems indicate that the tomato has been sitting around for a while. The tomato shouldn't have any soft spots. Buy tomatoes no more than a day or two before you plan to use them. This will ensure the best flavor and texture, providing the vendor has treated the tomato properly. When you shop, pick your tomatoes from the top of the pile, staying away from high tomato piles, because the bottom ones get bruised. Avoid refrigerated tomatoes. Tomatoes should never be refrigerated. Instead, store them at room temperature. They can stay for days on a kitchen counter. Refrigeration damages the membranes and flavor-producing enzymes in a tomato, causing its texture to become mealy. When you buy a tomato that is underripened, let it ripen in a cool place, such as the windowsill. Simply putting them in a brown bag or just resting on your counter also works well. The meaty beefsteak and oxheart tomatoes are best for sandwiches but are also great for a salad, as are all the different cherry tomatoes. I like heirloom tomatoes when in season; each varietal offers different textures and flavors. Some are sweeter, some more acidic, some vegetal, and some have a mineral aftertaste. Keep in mind that the red varieties of tomatoes tend to be more acidic than the yellow. Diversity of color also makes a tomato salad appealing.

CARROT AND APPLE SALAD

Insalata di Carote e Mele

This salad is not only delicious by itself but also a great platform for smoked meats or fish; it works well with trout, salmon, duck breast, and ham. Serve the proteins alongside the salad and you have a great appetizer or meal. It is a sandwich stuffer as well; instead of using mayonnaise or other fatty dressings, use this juicy salad. It is especially good on a sandwich of sliced turkey, chicken, or ham.

Serves 6

3 large carrots, peeled and julienned (about 2 cups)

2 Granny Smith apples, skin on, julienned (about 3 cups)

Juice of 1 orange

3 tablespoons extra-virgin olive oil

2 tablespoons chopped fresh Italian parsley

¼ teaspoon kosher salt

Freshly ground black pepper

Toss the carrots and apples in a salad bowl with the orange juice and olive oil. Sprinkle with the parsley, season with the salt and pepper, and toss again. Serve cold.

FENNEL AND GORGONZOLA SALAD

Insalata di Finocchio e Gorgonzola

Blue-cheese dressing over iceberg lettuce is common in steak houses around America. This is the Italian counterpart: fresh fennel with a Gorgonzola dressing. When you have some unfinished Gorgonzola in the refrigerator—because the longer it sits, the stronger it gets—think about making this salad dressing.

Serves 6

8 ounces Gorgonzola dolce, rind removed, crumbled

½ cup heavy cream

½ cup buttermilk

3 tablespoons white-wine vinegar

3 tablespoons extra-virgin olive oil

¼ teaspoon kosher salt

3 medium bulbs fennel, halved, cored, shaved on a mandoline

2 tablespoons chopped fresh Italian parsley

In a mini–food processor, combine the Gorgonzola, heavy cream, buttermilk, vinegar, oil, and salt. Pulse to make a chunky dressing.

In a large bowl, toss the shaved fennel and parsley. Drizzle the dressing over the contents, and toss well.

BELGIAN ENDIVE AND WALNUT SALAD

Insalata Belga e Noci

Crunch-crunch-crunch will end up as munch-munch-munch when this salad is served. Flavor is obviously crucial in food, and certainly this salad has flavor, but tactile sensation is also a very important factor in our food perception and appreciation. We want pasta al dente, celery crunchy, bread grilled. This salad has a lot of texture to enjoy.

Serves 6

3 tablespoons apple-cider vinegar

1 teaspoon Dijon mustard

1 teaspoon kosher salt

Freshly ground black pepper

5 tablespoons extra-virgin olive oil

6 heads Belgian endive, trimmed, cut on the bias into 1-inch-thick slices

2 apples, skin on, cored, sliced into thin half-moons

½ cup walnut pieces, toasted and chopped

In a small bowl, whisk together the vinegar, mustard, and salt, and season with black pepper. Whisk in the olive oil in a steady stream to make a smooth, emulsified dressing.

Toss the endive, apples, and walnuts together in a large serving bowl. Drizzle with the dressing, toss well, and serve immediately.

STRING BEANS, CAPERS, AND BASIL SALAD

Insalata di Fagiolini, Capperi, e Basilico

This is a refreshing salad, particularly in the summer months. Do play with the different kinds of string beans available in season. I love the flat Roman green varietal, but a mixture of green and yellow wax beans is delicious. This base salad can be enhanced to become a main course by adding canned tuna or sardines. It is also a great way to use leftover grilled fish or chicken.

Serves 6

¼ teaspoon kosher salt, plus more for the pot

1 pound string beans, trimmed

½ cup loosely packed fresh basil leaves

½ cup drained tiny capers in brine

2 tablespoons red-wine vinegar

2 tablespoons extra-virgin olive oil

Bring a large pot of salted water to boil. Add the string beans, and blanch until tender, about 7 to 8 minutes. Drain, and rinse to cool slightly.

Shred the basil. Put the string beans in a bowl, and toss with the capers and basil. Drizzle with the vinegar and oil, and season with the salt. Toss to coat, and serve slightly warm or at room temperature.

RUSTIC SALAD

Insalata Rustica

Sometimes I just want a salad for a meal, with lots of complex textures and flavors, and this is one of my favorites. Both refreshing and substantial, it delivers a wallop of flavor. Best of all, a lot of the ingredients can come straight from the cupboard.

Serves 6

1 pound russet potatoes, peeled, cut into 1-inch chunks

½ teaspoon kosher salt, plus more for the pot

6 anchovy fillets

2 tablespoons red-wine vinegar

1 tablespoon Dijon mustard

¼ cup extra-virgin olive oil

One 15-ounce can cannellini beans, drained and rinsed

1 bunch scallions, trimmed and chopped (about 1 cup)

6 cups baby arugula

2 hard-boiled eggs, peeled and quartered

In a medium saucepan, put the potatoes in salted cold water to cover. Bring to a simmer, and cook until tender but not mushy, about 10 to 12 minutes. Drain well.

While the potatoes cook, make the dressing. In a mini–food processor, pulse together the anchovies, vinegar, and mustard. With the processor running, drizzle in the olive oil to make a smooth, emulsified dressing.

When the potatoes are cooked, put them in a large bowl with the beans and scallions. Season with ¼ teaspoon salt, and toss with about three-quarters of the dressing.

In another bowl, toss the arugula with the remaining ¼ teaspoon salt and the remaining dressing. Add the eggs, and toss gently. Serve the salad on plates, with the arugula-egg mixture mounded on top of the potatoes.

CUCUMBERS WITH WHOLE WHEAT COUSCOUS

Cetrioli con Couscous Integrale

When you are looking for a sensible and delicious finger-food appetizer or a party snack, this salad, served with crackers or crostini, should be on your menu. It is refreshing, easy to make, and different from your neighbor's ordinary antipasti. It can be adapted to various kinds of cooked grains, such as barley, wheat, or even lentils. Just keep in mind the cooking time of the grain or legume. Serve it in Chinese soup spoons.

Serves 4 people

1 teaspoon kosher salt

1 cup whole-wheat couscous

1 pound Persian cucumbers, sliced ¼ inch thick

1 pint cherry tomatoes, halved

¾ cup plain Greek yogurt

¼ cup extra-virgin olive oil

¼ cup white-wine vinegar

2 tablespoons chopped fresh mint

In a small saucepan, bring 1¼ cups water and ½ teaspoon of the salt to a boil. Add the couscous. Remove from heat, cover tightly, and let it stand for 5 minutes to steam. Uncover, and fluff with a fork. Let cool.

When the couscous has cooled, add the cucumbers and tomatoes. In a small bowl, whisk together the yogurt, olive oil, vinegar, mint, and remaining ½ teaspoon salt. Pour over the salad, and toss well. Serve slightly chilled or at room temperature.

CHICKPEA SALAD

Insalata di Ceci

If you like canned tuna, this is a perfect recipe; the tuna becomes the dressing, and the vegetables and the legumes are the protagonists. I offer two options for the chickpeas: to reconstitute and cook the dry kind, or to buy the precooked canned ones. The salad will be good either way, but dry legumes and beans are so economical, as well as nutritionally valuable.

Serves 6

Two 15-ounce cans chickpeas, drained and rinsed, or ½ pound dry chickpeas, cooked

1 small red bell pepper, cut into thin strips

1 small yellow bell pepper, cut into thin strips

¼ cup thinly sliced red onion

¼ cup drained tiny capers in brine, chopped

¼ cup chopped pitted green olives

3 tablespoons chopped fresh Italian parsley

One 5-ounce can Italian tuna in oil, drained

3 tablespoons dry white wine

2 tablespoons white-wine vinegar

1 tablespoon Dijon mustard

1 garlic clove, peeled

¼ cup extra-virgin olive oil

In a large bowl, combine the chickpeas, bell peppers, red onion, capers, olives, and parsley.

In a mini–food processor, combine the tuna, white wine, vinegar, Dijon, and garlic. Pulse to combine. With the machine running, drizzle in the olive oil to make a smooth, emulsified dressing. Drizzle the dressing over the chickpeas, and toss to coat the salad.

QUICK TIP

To cook dry chickpeas, soak overnight in just enough water to cover. Drain the chickpeas and set them in a pot with abundant water to cover. Add 2 bay leaves and cook for about 45 minutes, until tender.

LENTIL COUNTRY SALAD

Insalata Contadina

Lentils are good in soup and with pasta, and I love making salads with them. This simple salad can be served warm or cold. It is always a welcoming dish, since there is something so inviting about it. I especially love this salad in the summer, when grilling or on a picnic.

Serves 6 to 8

1 pound dried lentils, rinsed and drained

1 medium onion, diced

2 cups peeled, diced carrots

2 cups diced celery

3 fresh bay leaves

¼ cup extra-virgin olive oil

6 ounces pancetta, diced

⅓ cup white wine

3 tablespoons white-wine vinegar

1 teaspoon kosher salt

3 tablespoons chopped fresh parsley

In a large saucepan, combine the lentils, onion, carrots, celery, bay leaves, and 2 quarts of water. Bring to a simmer, and cook until the lentils are tender, about 30 to 40 minutes. Drain, and remove the bay leaves. Scrape the lentils and vegetables into a serving bowl.

Meanwhile, in a medium skillet, heat 2 tablespoons of the olive oil over medium heat. Add the pancetta, and cook until crisp, about 4 minutes. Pour off most of the fat, and add the remaining 2 tablespoons of olive oil. Add the wine and vinegar, and season the dressing with the salt. Bring to a quick boil, then pour the dressing over the lentils. Toss with the parsley and serve.

TUNA, CORN, MUSHROOM, AND POTATO SALAD

Tonno, Mais, Funghi, e Patate

This is another one of those delicious salads where the only work you have to do is boil the potatoes and chop the parsley. It is great for summer picnics, a fast lunch, or when you have unexpected guests.

You can either use thawed frozen corn, or 2 cups of fresh corn kernels removed from the cob and blanched for 2 minutes.

Serves 6

1½ pounds Yukon Gold potatoes, cubed

½ teaspoon kosher salt, plus more for the pot

Three 5-ounce cans Italian tuna in olive oil, drained

1 cup drained marinated mushrooms, sliced

2 cups corn kernels (see headnote)

½ cup drained tiny capers in brine

5 tablespoons extra-virgin olive oil

¼ cup red-wine vinegar

3 tablespoons chopped fresh Italian parsley

¼ teaspoon crushed red-pepper flakes

Put the potatoes in a medium saucepan with salted water to cover. Bring to a simmer, and cook until potatoes are tender but not mushy, about 30 minutes. Drain well, and put in a large serving bowl.

Crumble in the tuna over the potatoes. Add the mushrooms, corn, and capers, and toss well. Drizzle with the oil and vinegar, and sprinkle with the parsley, salt, and red-pepper flakes. Toss well and serve.

BOILED ZUCCHINI SALAD WITH TUNA

Insalata di Zucchine e Tonno sott'Olio

There are many versions of tuna salad. It is typically Italian to add boiled or steamed vegetables to fish, eggs, or cheese and toss the whole mixture into an insalatone, *a big salad. Here just canned tuna in olive oil is added. Regular American white tuna can be used instead, but the results will be much better if you go with the Italian canned tuna packed in olive oil.*

Serves 6

¼ teaspoon kosher salt, plus more for the pot

1 pound medium zucchini, all about the same size

⅓ cup drained tiny capers in brine

Juice of 1 lemon

¼ teaspoon crushed red-pepper flakes

3 tablespoons extra-virgin olive oil

Two 5-ounce cans Italian tuna in oil, drained

Drop the whole zucchini into a pot of boiling salted water. Simmer until the zucchini is tender but not mushy, about 15 to 20 minutes. Drain, let cool slightly, then cut into ½-inch rounds. Put the sliced zucchini in a large serving bowl.

Toss the warm zucchini with capers, lemon juice, salt, and red-pepper flakes. Drizzle with olive oil, crumble in the tuna, and toss again.

SOUPS

Chicken stock is one of those basic recipes that you should make at home. It is simple to make and a sure sign that there is a caring and wise cook in the kitchen. Easy, economical, and a nutritional staple, it is at the base of so many nourishing and delicious dishes.

Once your chicken stock is made, you can turn it into delicious variations with the addition of a few ingredients.

- If you add to the chicken stock a few leaves of shredded fresh spinach, a whisked egg or two, and a sprinkle of some grated Grana Padano, and give it all a boil, you have *stracciatella alla romana.*
- If you top the hot chicken stock, in a plate with a slice of toast and a poached egg sprinkled with grated cheese, you have *zuppa alla pavese.*
- If you add some pieces of day-old bread to a pot of chicken soup, boil it until the bread falls apart, and sprinkle with some grated cheese and chopped parsley, you have *panada.*
- If you add rice and some fresh or frozen peas to chicken stock, boil until the rice is cooked, and add some cheese, you have *risi e bisi,* a typical Venetian dish.
- If you layer a casserole with blanched Savoy cabbage, day-old whole-wheat bread, and slices of provola cheese, soak it all with chicken stock, and bake it in a hot 400-degree oven for 45 minutes, you have a dense Sardinian *zuppa.*
- If you break some capellini in 1-inch pieces, add them to a boiling chicken stock, cook for 2 minutes, and add some Grana Padano, you have one of my favorite chicken soups.

The beauty of chicken stock is that you can make a big batch, letting it perk away while you are doing a thousand other things. Strain it, and freeze it in quarts, pints, or ice-cube trays. Once the soup cubes are frozen, pack them into ziplock bags, mark the date on all the containers, and you are ready to cook any recipe that requires stock.

CHICKEN STOCK

Brodo di Pollo

This is an easy, flavorful recipe for homemade chicken stock. It can be a meal in itself if you add some rice or pasta, or can be used as stock for various recipes in this book. Chicken stock is so easy to make: just put all ingredients in a stockpot and let it simmer.

Store the chicken stock leftovers in pint containers, label and date them, and freeze them. Chicken stock will keep in the freezer for 2 months for you to use as needed. I always have frozen chicken stock in the freezer in case the kids or friends unexpectedly drop over. I add some pastina, and the first course is ready.

What is of utmost importance in this recipe is that the chicken be top-quality free-range. I tell you to use chicken backs, necks, and wings, the parts that yield the most flavor. Make sure that, when the stock is done, you collect all the chicken meat off the bones, removing all the skin and fat, and add the meat to the soup when serving.

Makes about 4 quarts

4 pounds chicken backs, necks, and wings, trimmed of excess fat, rinsed well

1 large onion, cut into chunks

2 large carrots, peeled and cut into chunks

2 celery stalks, cut into chunks

5 garlic cloves, unpeeled

Handful fresh Italian parsley sprigs

1 teaspoon black peppercorns

Put the washed chicken parts in a large stockpot with 4 quarts of cold water. Bring to a boil, reduce to a simmer, and cook, skimming off the scum that rises to the surface, for 30 minutes.

Add the remaining ingredients, partially cover, and continue to simmer, skimming any additional fat or scum that comes to the surface, for 1½ hours.

Strain the stock through a fine sieve. If you are going to use the stock right away, let it settle for a few minutes, then use a spoon to skim off any fat that has risen to the surface. If you are not using it right away, cool to room temperature, then refrigerate. The fat will solidify on top, and you can easily scoop it off. When frozen, chicken stock will keep well for up to 2 months.

QUICK TIP

An excellent kitchen gadget to have is a fat separator and strainer. Skimming the fat off is good for clear stocks as well as gravies.

COUNTRY ONION SOUP

Cipollata alla Campagnola

This is one of those delicious soups you can make when you think you have nothing in the house to cook. The speck is wonderful because of its smoky flavor, but smoked bacon, prosciutto, or ham could be a good substitute.

Serves 6 to 8

¼ cup extra-virgin olive oil

2 pounds yellow onions, thinly sliced

1 teaspoon kosher salt

4 ounces speck, cut into matchsticks

2 tablespoons all-purpose flour

2 cups dry white wine

½ cup grated Grana Padano or Parmigiano-Reggiano, plus more for serving

Grilled or toasted country bread, for serving

In a large soup pot, heat the olive oil over medium heat. Add the onions, and season with the salt. Cook the onions until softened, about 10 minutes, then stir in the speck. Push the onions and speck to one side, and add the flour. Let the flour toast for a minute or two, then mix it into the onions.

Increase the heat to high, add the wine, and bring to a boil. Add 2 quarts of water, and bring to a rapid simmer. Cover, and cook until the onions are tender and the soup has thickened, about 40 minutes.

When you are ready to serve, turn off the heat and stir in the grated cheese. To serve the soup, place a piece of grilled bread in each bowl, and ladle the soup over the bread. Sprinkle with a little more grated cheese, and serve.

SPINACH AND CHICKPEA SOUP

Zuppa di Spinaci e Ceci

I love this soup with chickpeas, but the same recipe can be made with dry kidney or cannellini beans. I sometimes add pasta, such as ditalini or broken spaghetti, in the last 10 minutes of cooking, to give the soup more substance. You will need to have enough liquid in the pot to cook the pasta; if not, just add a cup or two of water, bring to a boil, season to taste, and then add the pasta. My grandmother would save all the little pieces of broken dry pasta and small amounts of different leftover pasta she had, and would throw it in the soup. So, when you have a little spaghetti, a little tubettini, a little fusilli left over, save it all as you go along, and then, when you decide to make zuppa, *just throw it all in and cook it.*

I sometimes substitute Swiss chard for the spinach, and it is also delicious.

Serves 8 or more

1 pound dried chickpeas, soaked overnight, drained

2 medium leeks, white and light green parts only, chopped (about 2 cups)

2 celery stalks, chopped (about 1 cup)

1 large carrot, peeled and chopped (about 1 cup)

2 fresh bay leaves

1 teaspoon crushed red-pepper flakes, or more to taste

2 large bunches leaf spinach, washed, tough stems removed (about 2½ pounds)

3 tablespoons kosher salt

⅓ cup extra-virgin olive oil

8 garlic cloves, peeled and sliced

Put the drained chickpeas in a large soup pot with the leeks, celery, carrot, bay leaves, and ½ teaspoon of the red-pepper flakes. Add 8 quarts of cold water, and bring to a rapid simmer. Partially cover, and cook until the chickpeas are almost tender, about 1½ hours.

Add the spinach and salt. Cover, and cook until the spinach is tender, 15 to 20 minutes more.

When the soup is ready, heat the olive oil in a medium skillet over medium heat. When the oil is hot, add the garlic and remaining ½ teaspoon red-pepper flakes. Cook until the garlic just begins to turn golden and is fragrant, about a minute, then ladle in a couple cups of soup, and stir to incorporate the flavored oil into the soup. Transfer the contents of the skillet to the large pot of soup, mix well, and serve.

TOMATO AND CLAM SOUP

Pappa al Pomodoro con Vongole

This dish has all the flavors of red clam sauce, and all the comforts of a tomato soup. For those days when you want to stay away from pasta and clam sauce, or don't feel like a creamy clam chowder, this is a delicious alternative. Serve it hot, or at room temperature in the summer, with some grilled crusty bread.

Serves 6 or more

6 tablespoons extra-virgin olive oil, plus more to finish

2 garlic cloves, peeled and sliced

2 dozen littleneck clams, washed and scrubbed

½ cup finely chopped onion

Two 28-ounce cans whole San Marzano tomatoes, crushed by hand (see page 78)

1 large fresh basil sprig

¼ teaspoon crushed red-pepper flakes

Kosher salt, to taste

2 cups day-old crustless bread cubes

In a large pot, over medium-high heat, put 2 tablespoons of the olive oil. When the oil is hot, add the garlic. Once the garlic is hot, add the clams and 1 cup of water. Cover, and simmer until the clams open, about 3 to 4 minutes. Remove the clams as they open, discarding any clams that don't open. Pass the cooking liquid through a strainer and reserve. Remove the clam meat from shells, and coarsely chop.

Meanwhile, in a soup pot, heat the remaining ¼ cup of olive oil over medium heat. Add the onion, and cook until tender, about 5 minutes. Add the tomatoes, basil, red-pepper flakes, 1 cup of water, and the reserved clam-cooking liquid. Taste, and season with salt. Bring to a simmer, and cook until thickened, about 20 minutes.

Add the bread cubes. Simmer, breaking up the bread cubes with a whisk to make a thick soup. Remove the basil. Stir in the chopped clams, and finish with a drizzle of olive oil.

Soup Tips

Soup is a simple course, but I like to give it the attention and the garnishes it deserves. I have one rule for serving soup, whether it's for a formal occasion or an everyday supper: hot soup in warm bowls, cold soup in chilled bowls. One way of serving hot soup is to bring it to the table, in a tureen or in the pot. Have the warm bowls stacked up, and ladle out and garnish each serving when everyone is seated. This is a great presentation as well as a safe delivery—no dribbling plates of soup plunked on the table.

Dress soup with a drizzle of extra-virgin olive oil and some grated Grana Padano, placing a bowl of the grated cheese on the table for anyone who wants more. I also suggest a pepper mill or a small bowl of crushed red pepper on the table, for people to add to the soup according to their taste. Some shredded fresh basil or parsley adds to the freshness and aroma. And if I am serving a vegetable- or bean-based soup, I like to whisk a teaspoon or two of basil pesto into it just before serving. So, next time you make pesto, make some extra and freeze it in an ice-cube tray. When it's frozen solid, store in ziplock bags and use the cubes for moments like these. While serving your soup, or next time you make Marinara Sauce (page 80), plop a pesto cube into the sauce as well.

When your soup is too thin and you want more body, add cooked pasta (such as ditalini), or cooked rice to it. Grilled bread or croutons will also do the trick and bring density when added to your soup.

TOASTED GRAIN SOUP

Minestra Abbrustolita

My grandmother cooked a similar soup; she would make it with regular flour milled from the wheat that she and my grandfather grew. I recall that the soup had a toasty flavor. At the end, just before serving it, my grandmother would whisk in two or three eggs gathered from her chickens. It was delicious. When I came across this recipe, I liked it even more for the diversity of grains used. When you make this soup, do try whisking in an egg or two and giving it a boil before serving. The soup will have more complexity and resemble Chinese egg-drop soup.

Serves 8 or more

½ cup barley

½ cup stoneground cornmeal

½ cup steel-cut oats

10 cups homemade Chicken Stock (page 55)

Kosher salt, to taste

8 ounces baby spinach

2 large eggs, beaten

½ cup grated Grana Padano or Parmigiano-Reggiano

In a food processor, grind the barley to a fine flour, and pour it into a bowl. Repeat this process with the cornmeal and oats. Heat the stock in a soup pot until it is simmering, and season with salt.

In a large skillet over low heat, toast the grains (all together), stirring constantly, until they're golden and smell very toasty, about 10 minutes, taking care not to burn. Scrape the toasted grains into a bowl to cool slightly.

Sprinkle the toasted grains into the simmering stock a little at a time, as you would cook polenta. Whisk until smooth. Bring to a rapid simmer, and cook until smooth and creamy, about 20 minutes.

Stir in the spinach, and cook until wilted, about 5 minutes. While stirring, drizzle the beaten eggs into the simmering soup to make thin strands or "rags," as you would make *stracciatella*. Turn off the heat, stir in the grated cheese, and serve.

SWISS CHARD AND LENTIL SOUP
Minestra di Lenticchie e Bietole

Swiss chard is a delicious vegetable, and it ranks at the top of the nutrition list. I cook with it a lot, but what I see often is a recipe calling for just the leaves of the chard. I always ask myself, what happens to the rest? Well, in this ideal recipe, you use everything, from leaves to stalks. Just clear off any blemished parts, and chop up all the rest for the soup. I recall that my grandmother Rosa would salvage even the blemished parts and serve them to the chickens, ducks, or pigs. Today that is probably not an easy option, but it did teach me to respect every crumb of food, not to waste a drop, and to recycle as much as possible.

Serves 8 or more (about 4 quarts)

4 ounces pancetta, chopped

3 garlic cloves, peeled and crushed

2 tablespoons extra-virgin olive oil

1 large onion, chopped (about 1½ cups)

1 medium carrot, peeled and chopped (about ½ cup)

1 celery stalk, chopped (about ½ cup)

One 28-ounce can whole San Marzano tomatoes, crushed by hand (see page 78)

2 fresh bay leaves

2 tablespoons kosher salt

2 bunches Swiss chard, cleaned, tough stems discarded, leaves and tender stems chopped (about 1½ pounds)

1 pound dried lentils, rinsed

In a mini–food processor, pulse the pancetta and garlic to make a smooth *pestata.* In a large soup pot, heat the olive oil over medium heat. Add the *pestata,* and cook until the fat has rendered, about 4 minutes. Add the onion, carrot, and celery, and cook until softened, about 5 minutes. Add the crushed tomatoes, and simmer for 5 minutes to concentrate the flavors. Add 6 quarts of water, the bay leaves, and salt. Simmer to develop the flavors, about 45 minutes.

Add the Swiss chard, and cook for 30 minutes. Add the lentils, and continue simmering until they are tender and the soup has thickened and is flavorful, another 40 minutes or so. Serve hot.

BREAD AND BASIL SOUP
Pancotto e Basilico

This is a historical soup. In some version or other it is cooked all over Italy, made in 10 minutes with basic ingredients from the cupboard. It is one of those heartwarming and delicious soups that you can cook for ten people or just make for yourself. Cooking does not always have to be complicated or time-consuming. Some of the simplest recipes using the smallest number of ingredients are the best achievements. I feel great when I make something so good with so little effort and in no time. This recipe is for one person, but you can see how easy it is to multiply the ingredients for your whole family.

You can also make this with stale bread cubes; just cook them a few minutes longer and break them up with a spoon or whisk.

Serves 1

1 tablespoon fine dried breadcrumbs

1 tablespoon chopped fresh basil
leaves

1 tablespoon grated Grana Padano or
Parmigiano-Reggiano

1 teaspoon unsalted butter or
extra-virgin olive oil

Kosher salt, to taste

Bring 1 cup of water to a simmer. When the water is simmering, stir in the breadcrumbs, and simmer until slightly thickened, about 5 minutes. Add the basil, and remove from the heat. Stir in the grated cheese and butter or oil. Season with salt and serve.

SEMOLINA AND ESCAROLE SOUP

Minestra di Semolino e Scarola

This is one of those too-good-to-be-true recipes. It is easy and quick to make, nourishing, and very tasty. Escarole and chicory are commonly used in Italy, but any vegetable, from spinach to zucchini to broccoli, will work perfectly in this soup. Just monitor the cooking time: some vegetables take a bit longer than others. Of course, if you want a more complete meal, you can always add shrimp, scallops, or shredded chicken. Just also keep in mind the cooking time of those proteins if you decide to add them.

Serves 6 to 8

4 tablespoons unsalted butter

1 bunch scallions, trimmed and chopped (about 1 cup)

8 cups Chicken Stock, preferably homemade (page 55)

Kosher salt, to taste

1 pound escarole, washed and chopped (about 2 small heads)

½ cup coarse semolina

Grated Grana Padano or Parmigiano-Reggiano, for serving

In a soup pot, over medium heat, melt the butter. When the butter is melted, add the scallions, and cook until wilted, about 4 minutes. Add the chicken stock, and bring to a simmer. Taste, and season with salt.

Add the escarole, and cook until wilted, about 10 minutes. Gradually whisk in the semolina, and simmer until the soup is thick and creamy, about 20 minutes. Serve hot, with grated cheese sprinkled on top.

Facing page, top: Semolina and Escarole Soup; middle: Oatmeal Biscuits (page 33); bottom: Toasted Grain Soup (page 61)

BARLEY SOUP

Orzetto

Vegetable-and-barley soup is one of my favorites, and I like to make a big pot of it, then freeze the extra. When I come home from the restaurants in the evening, a plate of this piping-hot soup and a glass of Morellino seals the day. It is always great to have a stash of goodies in the freezer, and nothing is better than having pints of good soup awaiting unexpected family members or guests who show up for dinner; a frozen soup or sauce saves the day. Just remember to package everything well and label and date all the foods you freeze, so you can rotate them properly.

Serves 8 or more

2 smoked ham hocks

¼ cup extra-virgin olive oil

2 cups peeled, cubed russet potatoes

2 medium leeks, white and light green parts only, chopped (about 2 cups)

1½ cups peeled, chopped carrots

1 cup chopped celery

1 pound split peas, rinsed

3 cups barley, rinsed

12 ounces baby spinach

2 cups corn kernels, fresh or frozen

2 tablespoons kosher salt

Put the ham hocks in a saucepan, and cover them with water. Bring to a simmer, and simmer for 10 minutes to remove some of the saltiness. Drain and rinse.

In a large soup pot, over medium heat, heat the olive oil. When the oil is hot, add the potatoes, and sauté until they begin to brown and stick to the bottom of the pan, about 5 minutes. Add the leeks, carrots, and celery, and sauté until everything is coated in the oil. Add 8 quarts of water, the split peas, and the ham hocks, and bring to a rapid simmer. Simmer, uncovered, until the peas have broken down, about 45 minutes.

Add the barley, and simmer until tender, about 45 minutes. The split peas should be broken down and have made the soup thick and creamy at this point. Add the spinach, corn, and salt, and simmer until the spinach is tender, about 10 minutes. Serve hot.

PASTA AND BEAN SOUP WHEN IN A HURRY

Pasta e Fagioli Veloce

Pasta e fagioli, *made the traditional way with dried beans, takes about 3 hours to cook. This delicious version is made in just 30 minutes. The beans used here are canned cooked beans, and you can either pass all the beans through a food mill or leave half of them whole to create more texture in the soup. This recipe is vegetarian, but you could add some sausages and make the meal more substantial. If adding sausages, cook them separately in boiling water for 15 minutes, then add to the boiling soup in the last 15 minutes of cooking.*

Serves 8 or more

Three 15-ounce cans cannellini beans, drained

½ cup extra-virgin olive oil

3 garlic cloves, peeled and crushed

2 tablespoons all-purpose flour

1 fresh rosemary sprig, needles stripped

2 teaspoons kosher salt

¼ teaspoon crushed red-pepper flakes

One 15-ounce can whole San Marzano tomatoes, crushed by hand (see page 78)

2 cups ditalini

2 tablespoons chopped fresh Italian parsley

In a blender, purée 2 cans of the beans with 1 cup water. Set aside.

In a large soup pot, heat the olive oil over medium heat. Add the garlic. Once the garlic is sizzling, sprinkle in the flour. Let the flour toast for a minute but not color; then add 3 quarts of water, the rosemary, salt, and red-pepper flakes. Bring to a boil, add the tomatoes, 1 cup slosh water from the tomato can, and the bean purée. Simmer until the soup thickens and is creamy and flavorful, about 30 minutes.

Add the ditalini and the final can of beans (not puréed), and simmer until the pasta is al dente. Stir in the parsley and serve.

> ### QUICK TIP
> To clean a blender, put a quarter of a blender-full of warm water in the dirty blender, and a drop of dishwashing liquid. Run the blender to give yourself a head start on the cleaning process.

LEGUME SOUP FROM ABRUZZO

"Virtù" Abruzzese

The name of this soup in Italian is virtù, *which means "virtue," and this soup surely contains many virtues, given all of the delightful legumes involved. The one thing to remember when making a soup with legumes is to give it enough time to slow-cook and perk away until the soup becomes velvety. In this recipe, the fava beans and chestnuts need to be cooked until they almost disintegrate.*

Serves 8 or more

2 smoked ham hocks

¼ cup extra-virgin olive oil

1 cup chopped onion

1 cup peeled, shredded carrot

1 cup chopped celery

1 cup canned whole San Marzano tomatoes, crushed by hand (see page 78)

1 pound dried fava beans, soaked overnight, drained, outer skin peeled (or use about ¾ pound already peeled dried favas if you can find them)

8 ounces chickpeas, soaked overnight and drained

3 cups coarsely chopped peeled chestnuts

3 fresh bay leaves

2 bunches Swiss chard, tough stems removed, leaves and tender stems and ribs shredded

8 ounces dried brown lentils

2 tablespoons kosher salt

In a medium saucepan, cover the ham hocks with cold water, bring to a simmer, and simmer for 10 minutes to remove some of the salt. Drain.

In a large soup pot, heat the olive oil over medium-high heat. Add the onion, carrot, and celery, and cook until softened, about 5 minutes. Add the tomatoes, favas, chickpeas, chestnuts, bay leaves, and 8 quarts of water. Bring to a simmer. Once the beans are simmering, add the drained ham hocks. Simmer the soup until all the beans are almost tender, about 1½ hours.

Add the chard, cover, and simmer until the chard wilts into the soup, about 15 minutes. Add the lentils, and cook until all the beans are very tender and the chestnuts have melted to make a creamy soup, about 30 minutes. Season with the salt. Serve hot.

QUICK TIP

Freeze soups and sauce in labeled ½-pint containers or in ziplock bags. Label and date the ziplock bag first, then place cold soup or sauce in bags. Seal the bags, lay them flat on a baking sheet, and freeze. Rotate items from the freezer, using the older items first.

CHICKPEA PURÉE SOUP

Crema di Ceci

This delicious purée works wonderfully on its own, with just a piece of grilled country bread to dip into it, but it is also delicious when seared shrimp or scallops are added to it. I like to make it with dried chickpeas; they are much more economical. All you need to do is soak them overnight and boil them. But when you are in a time pinch, the canned, cooked chickpeas will do. Drain them and proceed to pass them through the food mill.

Serves 8 or more

1 pound chickpeas, soaked overnight (see page 47)

6 garlic cloves, peeled and crushed

2 fresh bay leaves

2 fresh rosemary sprigs

1 tablespoon kosher salt

3 tablespoons extra-virgin olive oil, plus more for finish

Grilled country bread, for serving

Fresh basil leaves, shredded, for garnish

Drain the chickpeas, and put them in a pot with 3 quarts of cold water, the garlic, bay leaves, and rosemary. Simmer until the chickpeas are very tender, about 1 hour and 15 minutes.

Remove the bay leaves and rosemary and let cool before puréeing the chickpeas with an immersion blender or in a food processor (in batches). Pour soup back into a pot, add salt and oil, and return to a simmer before serving.

To serve, put a slice of grilled country bread in the bottom of each bowl, ladle the soup over the bread, and garnish with the shredded basil and a drizzle of olive oil.

BEAN SOUP "LE MARCHE" STYLE

Zuppa di Fagioli alla Marchigiana

One reason I love making soups is that you can include whatever legumes and vegetables you have handy; just leave them perking on the stove until they are velvety and delicious. They do not need a lot of attention, and they are best when they reflect the seasons. This hearty, healthy soup comes from the hills of the Le Marche region in Italy. Cabbage, especially Savoy cabbage, becomes very mellow and almost sweet when cooked in this soup. I love cabbage in a soup, especially in the fall and winter months, when it is seasonal and readily available. Cabbage is packed with nutrition and also quite economical.

Serves 8 or more

4 ounces slab bacon, cut into chunks

¼ cup extra-virgin olive oil

3 garlic cloves, peeled and crushed

2 medium carrots, peeled and cut into chunks

2 medium onions, cut into chunks

1 pound russet potatoes, peeled, cut into ½-inch chunks

One 28-ounce can whole San Marzano tomatoes, crushed by hand (see page 78)

1 pound dried kidney beans, soaked overnight, drained and rinsed

4 fresh bay leaves

1 medium head Savoy cabbage, shredded

2 pounds medium zucchini, diced

2 tablespoons kosher salt

In a food processor, process the bacon to a smooth-textured paste, or *pestata.* In a large soup pot, heat the olive oil over medium heat. Add the bacon paste, and begin to render the fat. In the same food processor, combine the garlic, carrots, and onions. Process to another smooth *pestata,* and add to the rendered bacon. Cook until the *pestata* begins to dry out and stick to the bottom of the pan, about 5 minutes. Add the potatoes, tomatoes, and 6 quarts of water. Bring to a simmer, then add the beans and bay leaves. Cover, and cook for 30 minutes.

Uncover, add the cabbage, and cook for another 20 minutes, until the cabbage has wilted and made room in the soup for the zucchini. Add the zucchini, and continue to simmer the soup until the beans are very tender, another 1 to 1½ hours. Season with the salt. Serve hot.

Facing page, top: Bean Soup "Le Marche" Style; bottom: Baked Toast Sandwiches (page 29)

CREAM OF CELERY ROOT SOUP

Crema di Sedano Rapa

Celery root is an underused root vegetable. I love it. Root vegetables are available when other green vegetables are not, and this one is economical, has longevity in the refrigerator, and has a very pronounced, clean flavor. I like celery root cooked as well as raw in salads. And I love it in this soup!

Serves 6

8 cups Chicken Stock, preferably homemade (page 55)

2 tablespoons unsalted butter

2 tablespoons extra-virgin olive oil

1 cup chopped onion

4 garlic cloves, peeled and crushed

2 tablespoons all-purpose flour

2 pounds celery root, peeled and chunked

Kosher salt to taste

Bring the chicken stock to a simmer in a saucepan.

In a soup pot, melt the butter in the olive oil over medium heat. When the butter is melted, add the onion and garlic, and cook until softened, about 5 minutes. Sprinkle in the flour, and stir to form a smooth roux with no clumps of flour. Cook, without browning the flour, for a few minutes to remove the raw flour smell and taste.

Slowly add the hot chicken stock, whisking to combine it with the roux. Add the celery root, and season with salt. Bring to a simmer, and cook until the celery root is very tender, about 30 to 40 minutes. Purée in batches in a blender, or right in the pot with an immersion blender. Return to a simmer and serve.

MILLET SOUP

Minestra di Miglio

Millet, a small seed gathered from grasses, is one of the oldest grains grown by man. As nutritionally wonderful as it is environmentally sound, it grows in difficult environments, even in drought areas, and has a fast cycle of growth. It is great in soups as well as in salads. Seeds are the basis of new life and hold lots of nourishment, so it makes sense to use them in cooking. Sesame seeds, poppy seeds, caraway seeds, pumpkin seeds, and nuts are all delicious.

Serves 6

8 cups Chicken Stock, preferably homemade (page 55)

Kosher salt, to taste

10 ounces pearl millet

5 ounces baby spinach, chopped

4 tablespoons unsalted butter, in small pieces

½ cup grated Grana Padano or Parmigiano-Reggiano

Bring the chicken stock to a simmer in a soup pot, and lightly salt.

In a skillet, toast the millet, stirring constantly, until fragrant, about 5 minutes. Add the toasted millet to the stock, and continue simmering until tender, about 20 minutes.

Add the baby spinach, and simmer until tender, about 3 minutes. Remove the soup pot from the heat, and let sit a few minutes so the millet absorbs a little of the stock. Whisk in the butter a few pieces at a time. Stir in the grated cheese and serve.

COUNTRY-STYLE FAVA SOUP

Fave alla Contadina

Pot meals like this one are delicious and practical: you can serve six or more and have some left for freezing. To add more texture and volume to the soup, you can add a cup of rice or 2 cups of pasta in the last 10 to 20 minutes of cooking. If you have never cooked with dry fava beans, this will be a revelation, and I am sure they will become part of your dry-legume shopping in the future.

Serves 8 or more

¼ cup extra-virgin olive oil

4 garlic cloves, peeled and sliced

1 large onion, chopped (about 1½ cups)

1 bulb fennel, halved, cored, and chopped (about 1½ cups)

1 large carrot, peeled and chopped (about 1 cup)

3 tablespoons tomato paste

1 pound shelled dried favas, soaked overnight and drained

1½ pounds pork spareribs (for a meatier soup, use 3 pounds), cut into 2-rib pieces

1 bunch Swiss chard (about 1 pound), chopped

2 tablespoons kosher salt

1½ cups ditalini

Heat the olive oil in a large soup pot over medium heat. When the oil is hot, add the garlic. Once the garlic begins to sizzle, add the onion, fennel, and carrot. Cook until the vegetables begin to soften, about 6 minutes. Clear a space in the pot, and add the tomato paste. Toast the tomato paste for a minute or two, then stir it into the vegetables. Add 6 quarts of cold water, the drained favas, and the ribs, and simmer until the ribs are tender and the favas begin to melt into the soup, about 1 hour.

Add the Swiss chard and salt. Simmer until the chard is tender, another 30 minutes or so. Add the ditalini, and cook until it is al dente, according to package directions. Serve hot.

> ### QUICK TIP
> If you have a big bunch of washed leafy greens, you can place them in the dish rack next to the sink to drain.

FAVA BEAN SOUP WITH DRIED FIGS

Zuppa di Fave e Fichi Secchi

Most people are familiar with the fresh green favas in their pods, but fava is a legume, and, like all beans in southern Italy, when they are abundant, in season, they are shucked and dried for the winter. When dry fava beans are cooked long enough, they disintegrate and make a very creamy, velvety soup. The addition of the chopped figs gives this soup a unique, delicious, sweet tinge.

Serves 8 or more

2 pounds dried fava beans, soaked overnight and peeled

2 cups peeled, shredded carrot

2 cups sliced white and light green parts of leeks

2 cups chopped celery

8 ounces dried figs, finely chopped

8 fresh sage leaves

4 fresh bay leaves

2 tablespoons kosher salt

¼ cup extra-virgin olive oil

Croutons or toasted or grilled bread, for serving

In a large soup pot, combine 6 quarts of cold water, the peeled favas, carrots, leeks, celery, figs, sage, and bay leaves. Bring to a simmer, and cook until the favas are very tender and have partially dissolved to make a creamy soup.

Season with the salt, and stir in the olive oil. Serve the soup with croutons or grilled bread floating on top.

SAUCES

Which Tomatoes Should You Use to Make Marinara Sauce?

Fresh tomatoes are always delicious and should be used when in season. However, there are excellent canned tomatoes that allow the home cook to create wonderful tomato dishes all year round.

When you're stocking your pantry with canned tomatoes, San Marzano (if available) is always the best choice. Grown in the Campania region of Italy, these sexy tomatoes are the best for sauce, because they are very meaty, have minimal juice, and fewer seeds than other tomatoes. (Seeds have tannins and tend to make your tomato sauce bitter.) If you do not have access to the canned San Marzano, although they are grown in America as well, choose canned plum tomatoes, which are in the same family as the San Marzano. They also have a lot of pulp and not too much juice or too many seeds, and they create a dense and sweet tomato sauce.

Get in the habit of tasting the tomatoes as soon as you open the can, and you will be able to tell which ones you like best; then stick to that brand. Keep in mind that tomatoes are packed seasonally and may vary from year to year, even from the same packer.

To make the sauce, after opening the can, crush the tomatoes with your hands or with a vegetable mill. I do not like to cook with canned crushed tomatoes or tomato chunks in purée.

If you are using fresh seasonal tomatoes, peel and seed the tomatoes before making the sauce. Bring a pot of water to a boil, then fill a bowl with ice water (make sure the bowl is big enough to hold all of the tomatoes and the water). With a paring knife, cut the cores out of the tomatoes and cut a small "x" in the opposite end. Place the tomatoes in the boiling water and leave them in for just a couple of minutes. You should see the skin begin to loosen. Fish the tomatoes out, and place them in the bowl of ice water; let them sit there for 5 minutes. Peel the skins off the blanched tomatoes. To remove the seeds, cut the blanched and peeled tomato in half—lengthwise for plum tomatoes, and crosswise for round tomatoes. Gently squeeze out the seeds with your hands, over a sieve; discard the seeds, and retrieve the pulp and juice. Crush the pulp, and proceed to make the sauce.

MARINARA SAUCE

Sugo alla Marinara

This is one of those sauces that you must try. Once you do, I assure you that you will make it one of your family's standard recipes. It is quick, simple, and nutritionally sound, and this sauce is at the base of many other recipes.

You can double or triple this recipe for big dinners, or you can freeze it and use it in future meals. It keeps in the freezer for a month or two.

Makes about 3½ cups, enough for
1 pound of pasta

¼ cup extra-virgin olive oil

7 garlic cloves, peeled and sliced

One 28-ounce can whole San Marzano tomatoes, crushed by hand
(see page 78)

Pinch crushed red-pepper flakes

1 teaspoon kosher salt

1 fresh basil sprig

In a large skillet, over medium heat, heat the olive oil. When the oil is hot, add the garlic. Once the garlic is sizzling, add the tomatoes, slosh out the can with 1 cup water, and add that as well. Sprinkle in the red-pepper flakes, and season with the salt. Submerge the basil sprig in the sauce.

Simmer the sauce until it is slightly thickened, about 15 minutes. Discard the basil.

DIP FOR VEGETABLES
Condimento per Cruditè

Crunchy fresh vegetables with a delicious dip are a great way to start a meal. This dip is easy to make and uses fresh ingredients—no packaged stuff here. This can also become a dressing for a salad or a spread for a sandwich.

Makes about 2½ cups

2 garlic cloves, peeled and finely chopped

3 large egg yolks

½ teaspoon kosher salt

1½ cups extra-virgin olive oil (a light, fruity one)

Juice of ½ lemon

Freshly ground black pepper, to taste

In a food processor or in a bowl, whisk together the garlic and egg yolks, then whisk in the salt. Add the olive oil in a slow and steady stream, whisking all the while, until all of the oil is incorporated and you have a pale-yellow, emulsified dressing. Whisk in the lemon juice and pepper.

Cover, and refrigerate for several hours to blend the flavors before serving. If needed, thin with a little water.

Smell the Herbs

In some cultures, the aromas that waft through the kitchen are those of spices, but in an Italian kitchen, the aromas largely come from fresh herbs. Most spices grow in the earth's tropical belt, whereas herbs mostly grow in temperate zones. The Mediterranean offers the ideal climate for aromatic herbs. But food cultures have intermingled herbs and spices across continents for centuries. A case in point is the explosion of fresh herbs in the American kitchen today.

When I was a young apprentice at my great-aunt's apron strings in Italy, I recall that for every pot that went on the stove there was an herb somewhere in the garden to match. Some herbs were better cooked, and others were better added to the finished dish. Rosemary, bay leaves, and thyme were mostly used for long cooking, because their oils are extracted slowly out of their leaves in the process. Sage, oregano, and marjoram need very little cooking time to extract their aroma. Basil, parsley, and mint are usually tossed raw into food at the last minute for their explosive fresh aromas.

When I cook, not only do I add fresh herbs to my food, but I love to crush herbs in my hands and then inhale their perfumes. It invigorates me, it refreshes me, and I get a good sense of what I am adding to the pot.

FRESH MINT SAUCE

Salsa Fresca

This simple dressing is refreshing and tasty, and it beautifully dresses boiled potatoes or boiled eggs. Use it also to dress any boiled or steamed vegetable, such as zucchini, broccoli, or cauliflower. Steaming is a healthy way to approach cooking vegetables, but they need not be bland; topping them with this vibrant sauce will bring them alive.

Makes enough for 6 halved hard-boiled eggs or 1 pound boiled potatoes (6 servings)

1 packed cup fresh parsley leaves

½ packed cup fresh mint leaves

2 tablespoons white-wine vinegar

½ teaspoon kosher salt

¼ cup extra-virgin olive oil

In a food processor, combine the parsley, mint, vinegar, and salt. Pulse once or twice to combine, then, with the machine running, drizzle the olive oil in a slow, steady stream to make a smooth dressing. Serve over halved hard-boiled eggs, or toss with chunked boiled potatoes still warm from cooking.

HAMBURGER SAUCE

Salsa all'Americana

Ketchup is the all-American condiment, but instead of squeezing the bottle, try making your own version. Note that this recipe can easily be doubled. The ketchup will keep in the refrigerator for a week or so.

Makes about 2 cups

1 cup finely chopped onion

½ cup peeled, shredded carrot

½ cup finely chopped celery

2 teaspoons fresh thyme leaves, chopped

1 teaspoon mustard powder

½ teaspoon cayenne

⅛ teaspoon ground cinnamon

2 tablespoons tomato paste

1 tablespoon honey

2 teaspoons kosher salt

One 28-ounce can whole San Marzano tomatoes, crushed by hand (see page 78)

¼ cup red-wine vinegar

In a medium saucepan, combine the onion, carrot, celery, thyme, mustard, cayenne, cinnamon, tomato paste, honey, and salt. Stir in 1½ cups of water, and bring to a simmer. Simmer until the vegetables begin to soften, about 5 minutes.

Add the crushed tomatoes and vinegar. Simmer until the sauce is very thick and flavorful, about 30 minutes.

ONION VERMOUTH SAUCE

Salsa al Vermut

When chicken breasts are too dry and fish fillets seem tasteless, try this quick, delicious sauce. It can also become a marinade for leftover chicken and fish. Set the leftovers in the sauce, and let them marinate in the refrigerator; eat them the next day, at room temperature, heated, or in a sandwich.

Serves 6

3 tablespoons extra-virgin olive oil

3 cups sliced onions

2 fresh bay leaves

1 teaspoon kosher salt

2 cups dry vermouth

2 tablespoons lemon juice

1 tablespoon cold unsalted butter

1 tablespoon chopped fresh Italian parsley

In a large skillet, over medium heat, heat the olive oil. When the oil is hot, add the onions and bay leaves, and season with the salt. Cook until onions are slightly wilted, about 5 minutes.

Add the vermouth and lemon juice, and bring to a simmer. Cook until onions are very tender, about 40 minutes. Increase the heat to bring to a boil, and reduce until the sauce is thick. Whisk in the cold butter and parsley, and serve or use as a marinade. This sauce will keep well in the freezer for 3 to 4 weeks, but don't add the parsley till you're ready to use it.

VEGETABLES
AND SIDES

Love Your Vegetables:
Easier to Cook Than You Think

I love cooking with and eating vegetables. Unfortunately, if one food category is lacking on the American table, it is vegetables. The Italian cuisine, on the other hand, is all about vegetables—especially seasonal vegetables. Appetizers are largely made up of pickled, grilled, marinated, or steamed vegetables. The diversity and beauty of Italian soups is in the legumes and vegetables that enrich them. The repertoire of pasta and risotto dishes would diminish by half if there were no vegetables.

For me as a chef, it is ever more exciting to see all the farmers' markets that are sprouting up across America. Burgeoning varieties of vegetables, especially the ethnic varieties, are available today. In the Italian category, there is broccoli rabe, fennel, radicchio, cavolo nero (kale), cardoons, and squash cocuzza with its tendrils. Simply braised with extra-virgin olive oil and garlic, these vegetables will turn into a delectable dish or can be served as a dressing for pasta. If you stuff these braised vegetables between two slices of crusty bread, the juiciness of the vegetables will dress the bread without the need of any mayonnaise or creamy dressing, and make a splendid sandwich. And simple, seemingly mundane vegetables can turn into glorious treats with a little imagination: Celery, Potatoes, and Tomatoes (page 93), Celery au Gratin (page 104), Tasty Cauliflower (page 99), Potatoes Baked in Beer (page 92), or Veggie Meatballs (page 115). Stuffing vegetables elevates them to a gratifying and fulfilling main-course status, such as Stuffed Eggplant Puglia Style (page 109) Gluttonous Tomatoes (page 106), Savory Stuffed Peppers (page 110), Zucchini Parmigiana (page 111), and Eggplant and Rice Parmigiana (page 112).

Another simple and delicious way to cook vegetables is to *strascinare* them, no special recipe needed. To *strascinare,* in Italian, is to drag your cleaned and washed vegetables in a pot with crushed garlic and olive oil, with a sprinkle of salt and some crushed red pepper (if you like the heat, as I do). It is also nutritious: you do not waste any of those flavors or nutritional elements in a big pot of water, because it all stays in the skillet. Another plus is having only one pot and lid to wash. Covering the skillet allows the vegetables to soften in their own moisture as the liquid evaporates gradually and caramelization happens. All you need is a heavy-bottomed skillet or pan large enough to hold all your vegetables in a single layer with room to move, so every piece can cook and caramelize.

What you need to bring to cooking all foods, not just these "dragged" vegetables, are your senses and your awareness of what's going on in the pan. Even when it's covered, the smells and sounds coming from a pan on the stove have something to tell you: how fast something is cooking, whether it is fully cooked, and when cooking is turning to burning. Become familiar with the techniques you use and the foods you cook. Learn to respond to the process with your senses, and ultimately you will be in control of the process.

No recipe can give you that sensibility. The judgment is up to you, the cook. Become confident, and master the simple but powerful process of cooking.

MASHED POTATOES AND FAVA BEANS

Purea di Fave e Patate

When you crave the comfort of mashed potatoes but want a bit of something more, this is the way to go. Favas are best in the late spring, but frozen favas are good, and lima beans make a fine substitute when no favas are to be found. This recipe works with other vegetables as well. Mashed potatoes with Swiss chard is an old family favorite; spinach and string beans also work well in this recipe. So, as I always tell you, do not be shy about substituting whatever you have in your refrigerator. Take my recipe and run with it.

Serves 6

2 pounds russet potatoes, peeled

2 garlic cloves, peeled and crushed

2 fresh bay leaves

2 pounds fava beans, shelled and peeled (about 2 cups)

1 teaspoon kosher salt

⅓ cup extra-virgin olive oil, plus more for serving

½ cup grated Grana Padano or Parmigiano-Reggiano

Put the potatoes, garlic, and bay leaves in a pot with water to cover. Bring to a simmer, and cook until the potatoes are just beginning to become tender, 10 to 12 minutes or more, depending on size.

Add the favas, and cook until both the potatoes and favas are tender, about 8 to 10 minutes more.

Drain. Remove and discard the bay leaves. Over low heat, coarsely mash the potatoes and favas with the salt and olive oil. Turn off the heat, stir in the grated cheese, and serve, drizzled with a little olive oil on top.

SAVORY POTATOES

Patate Appetitose

Who doesn't like roasted potatoes? Well, this recipe is all about the delicious flavor of roasted potatoes packed with a Mediterranean punch. It is a great accompaniment to roasted fish, grilled chicken, or lamb chops. I also suggest you try them for brunch, paired with fried or poached eggs.

Serves 6

1½ pounds Yukon Gold potatoes, peeled, sliced ½ inch thick

1 large onion, thinly sliced

2 teaspoons dried oregano

1¼ teaspoons kosher salt

6 tablespoons extra-virgin olive oil

1 pound cherry tomatoes, halved through the top

3 tablespoons grated Grana Padano or Parmigiano-Reggiano

Preheat the oven to 400 degrees F. In a large bowl, toss together the potatoes, onion, 1 teaspoon of dried oregano, and 1 teaspoon of salt. Drizzle with ¼ cup of the olive oil, and toss to coat. Spread the potato-and-onion mixture evenly in the bottom of a 15-by-10-inch or other large baking dish.

In the same bowl, toss together the tomatoes, remaining teaspoon of oregano, remaining ¼ teaspoon of salt, and the grated cheese. Drizzle with the remaining 2 tablespoons of olive oil, and toss to coat. Sprinkle the tomatoes evenly over the potatoes. Bake until the potatoes are cooked through and crusty and any liquid has evaporated from the baking dish, about 40 to 45 minutes.

POTATOES BAKED IN BEER

Patate alla Birra

Serves 6

2 tablespoons unsalted butter, at room temperature

4 ounces pancetta, cut into cubes

2 pounds russet potatoes, peeled, sliced into ½-inch rounds

1 teaspoon kosher salt

2 medium onions, thinly sliced

1 cup beer (lager)

1 cup heavy cream

Preheat the oven to 400 degrees F. Grease a 15-by-10-inch baking dish with the butter. In a mini–food processor, process the pancetta to a paste. In a large bowl, toss the potatoes with ½ teaspoon of the salt and the pancetta paste.

Spread the sliced onions on the bottom of the baking dish, and season with remaining ½ teaspoon salt. Layer the potatoes on top. In a spouted measuring cup, combine the beer and cream and pour over the potatoes. Cover with foil, and bake until bubbly, about 30 minutes. Uncover, and cook until the potatoes are browned and tender, about 20 minutes more.

CELERY, POTATOES, AND TOMATOES

Sedano, Patate, e Pomodori

This recipe uses some of the basic and simple ingredients found in most refrigerators, transforming them into a dish full of power. The potatoes take on the flavor of the celery and the acidity of the tomatoes. Combining potatoes with other vegetables is a great way to control your starch intake.

Serves 6

3 tablespoons extra-virgin olive oil

1½ pounds Yukon Gold or russet potatoes, peeled, cut into ½-inch cubes

4 celery stalks, cut into ½-inch pieces

2 beefsteak tomatoes, seeded, chopped into ½-inch pieces

½ teaspoon kosher salt

½ cup halved pitted green olives

In a large nonstick skillet, heat the olive oil over medium heat. When the oil is hot, add the potatoes. Cook until browned on all sides, about 5 to 7 minutes. Add the celery, and cook until softened, about 5 minutes.

Add the tomatoes, and season with the salt. Add the olives, and cook just until the tomatoes begin to break down but still retain their shape, about 5 minutes.

ONIONS AND CAPERS IN MARSALA

Cipolle e Capperi al Marsala

This recipe is the perfect example of how to build flavors into an otherwise underappreciated vegetable. Onions are at the base of many food preparations, from salads to soups to pasta and all kinds of meat and fish, but rarely are they featured in a recipe. Here they are the star, and a delicious one at that. This is a great appetizer or side dish, and a hit on any buffet table.

Serves 6

12 boiling onions, peeled but left whole

12 whole cloves

4 tablespoons unsalted butter, cut into pieces

2 cups dry Marsala wine

6 fresh thyme sprigs

2 fresh rosemary sprigs

6 garlic cloves, peeled and crushed

½ teaspoon kosher salt

½ cup drained tiny capers in brine

Stick a clove in each onion, and put the onions in a saucepan just large enough to fit them all snugly. Drop in the butter. Pour in the Marsala wine and 2 cups of water. Stick in the herb sprigs and garlic. Bring to a boil, cover, then simmer for another 20 minutes.

Add the salt, then simmer, uncovered, until onions are very soft all the way through, about 35 minutes, adding the capers in the last 10 minutes.

Remove onions to a serving dish. Strain the sauce back into the pan and reduce it until it's thick enough to glaze the onions. Pour it over the onions and serve.

Facing page, top: Onions and Capers in Marsala; bottom: Peppers Piedmontese (page 9)

Feel Freshness

Vegetables, fruits, fish, and meats will speak to your touch, so stay tuned and listen. I know that I understand the freshness of food much better when I have handled it. I can tell if meat is stringy and tough by pressing it with my fingers. I can tell how fresh fish is by how firm it is to my touch. I can tell that vegetables are fresh when they are firm and crisp; an artichoke squeaks under my fingers, string beans snap when bent, peppers squirt when broken into, and an eggplant is shiny and firm to the touch. It might be hard to do all this while shopping, but once you are in your kitchen you can affirm the freshness of the products you bought and make appropriate shopping choices next time.

TASTY CAULIFLOWER
Cavolfiori Gustosi

This recipe is for cauliflower, but the dressing can be used with other boiled or steamed vegetables, such as potatoes, zucchini, and parsnips.

Serves 6

1 large head cauliflower (about 2 pounds), broken into small florets

10 large fresh basil leaves

8 anchovies

8 cornichons

2 tablespoons drained tiny capers in brine

2 tablespoons chopped fresh parsley leaves

2 tablespoons red-wine vinegar

1 tablespoon Dijon mustard

¼ cup extra-virgin olive oil

Bring a large pot of water to boil. Add the cauliflower, and cook until tender, about 15 minutes.

Meanwhile, in a mini–food processor, combine the basil, anchovies, cornichons, capers, parsley, vinegar, and mustard. Slowly drizzle in the olive oil, pulsing to make a chunky dressing. When cauliflower is tender, drain well and toss with the dressing. Serve warm or at room temperature.

BRAISED CABBAGE WITH PROSCIUTTO

Verza e Prosciutto

This simple recipe can be prepared with regular or Savoy cabbage. It is best when the cabbage is in season and abundant. Bacon can be substituted for the prosciutto, and smoked bacon will add an additional dimension of flavor. I sometimes substitute apple cider vinegar for the white wine vinegar.

Serves 6

⅓ cup extra-virgin olive oil

6 garlic cloves, peeled and crushed

3 ounces thickly sliced prosciutto, cut into strips

1 medium head Savoy cabbage, cored and thinly sliced (about 2 pounds)

1 cup white wine

½ cup white wine vinegar

1 teaspoon kosher salt

In a Dutch oven, heat the olive oil over medium heat. When the oil is hot, add the garlic. Once the garlic is sizzling, add the prosciutto, and cook until the fat has rendered. Add the cabbage, wine, and vinegar. Season with the salt, and increase the heat to medium-high. Cover, and simmer until the cabbage is completely wilted, about 20 minutes.

Lower the heat, uncover, and simmer until the sauce has reduced and the cabbage is very tender, about 15 minutes more.

When to Salt Vegetables

When steaming or boiling vegetables, do not add salt before cooking. Salt the vegetables immediately after they are cooked and still hot. Once drained, toss them gently with medium-coarse salt. Does it make much of a difference? Indeed it does. Instead of making a saline solution out of the boiling water, which permeates the vegetable throughout, you allow the vegetable to retain its pure vegetable flavor. Then you highlight it by adding salt at the end. The vegetables that best respond to this method are string beans, broccoli, and zucchini, but I find it also works with cabbage, beets, chard, and other greens.

MINT STRING BEANS

Fagiolini alla Menta

Everybody is familiar with string beans dressed with butter, but the addition of one herb, mint, re-creates the dish so it has a new and fresh taste. Use this simple addition for zucchini, peas, cauliflower, and others of your favorite vegetables.

Serves 6

1 pound string beans, trimmed

3 tablespoons unsalted butter

1 loosely packed cup fresh mint leaves, chopped

¼ teaspoon kosher salt

Bring a large pot of water to a boil. Add the beans, and blanch until tender, about 8 to 10 minutes. Remove to an ice bath or bowl of cold water.

Meanwhile, in a large skillet, melt the butter over medium heat. Add the mint and salt. Add the blanched beans, toss, and cook for a minute, to coat the beans with the butter and blend the flavors.

CELERY AU GRATIN

Sedani al Gratin

Celery is not used nearly enough. This simple preparation will have you thinking more often about celery as a delicious side dish or appetizer.

Serves 6

1½ pounds celery (about 1½ heads)

1 cup panko breadcrumbs

1 cup grated Grana Padano or Parmigiano-Reggiano

5 tablespoons unsalted butter, cut into small cubes

½ teaspoon kosher salt

2 medium tomatoes, diced

Preheat the oven to 400 degrees F. Bring a large pot of water to boil. Trim the celery, and cut the stalks into 2-inch lengths. Blanch in the boiling water until the celery is almost tender but not floppy, about 7 minutes. Drain, reserving ½ cup of the celery-cooking water. In a bowl, mix panko and Grana Padano together.

Grease a 9-by-13-inch baking dish with 2 tablespoons of the butter. Layer half of the celery, all facing one direction, and season with ¼ teaspoon salt. Then dot with 1 tablespoon of the remaining butter, and pour over it the reserved celery-cooking water. Layer the remaining celery, scatter the diced tomatoes on top, and season with the remaining ¼ teaspoon of salt. Sprinkle with the cheese crumbs, and dot with the remaining butter. Bake until the celery is tender and the crumbs are crisp and golden brown, about 30 minutes.

BAKED FENNEL WITH SAGE

Finocchio alla Salvia

Fennel is not enjoyed as much in the United States as it is in Italy, perhaps because of the unfamiliarity of preparing it. Fennel is as easy to clean as an onion, and once it is baked it is as mellow as sweet potatoes, but the extra bonus is the licorice taste that it delivers. In this recipe, coupled with sage and Italian Fontina cheese, it is luscious.

Raw fennel eaten at the end of a meal is used often in southern Italy as a digestive.

Serves 6

½ teaspoon kosher salt, plus more
  for the pot

3 bulbs fennel, trimmed (about
  2 pounds)

8 ounces grated Italian Fontina

½ cup grated Grana Padano or
  Parmigiano-Reggiano

2 tablespoons unsalted butter

6 large fresh sage leaves, chopped

Preheat the oven to 425 degrees F. Bring a large pot of salted water to a boil. Halve and core the fennel, and slice it ½ inch thick. Add the slices of fennel to the boiling water, and blanch until tender, about 15 to 20 minutes. Drain and rinse.

In a medium bowl, toss together the Fontina and grated Grana Padano. Butter a 9-by-13-inch baking dish. Spread in the blanched fennel, and season with the salt. Scatter the chopped sage over the top, and sprinkle with the grated cheese. Bake until browned and bubbly, about 20 to 25 minutes.

GLUTTONOUS TOMATOES

Pomodori Ghiotti

This is a perfect appetizer or lunch dish, but I love making it for breakfast, especially when you have a houseful of people. Set the tomatoes in the oven; when they're done, bring the roasting pan of bubbling egg-filled tomatoes to the table; there will be a run on them.

Serves 4

4 large firm tomatoes, halved at the
  belly

2 cups stale ½-inch country-bread
  cubes, crusts removed

⅔ cup grated Grana Padano or
  Parmigiano-Reggiano

2 tablespoons chopped fresh Italian
  parsley

3 tablespoons extra-virgin olive oil

2 teaspoons dried oregano

1 teaspoon kosher salt

4 large eggs

Preheat the oven to 375 degrees F. Scoop out the seeds and pulp of the tomatoes over a fine strainer, making tomato shells. Press the seeds and pulp through the strainer and collect the juice. You should have about ¾ cup tomato juice.

In a large bowl, combine the bread cubes, ⅓ cup grated cheese, parsley, 2 tablespoons of olive oil, 1 teaspoon dried oregano, and ½ teaspoon salt, and toss well.

Grease a 9-by-13-inch baking dish with the remaining tablespoon of olive oil, and set the tomato shells inside. Season the inside of the tomatoes with the remaining ½ teaspoon salt. Pack the tomatoes with the stuffing, making an indentation in each mound of stuffing large enough to break an egg into. Pour tomato juice into the bottom of the pan (but not on the tomatoes). If you like, add a little extra stuffing between the tomatoes. Cover with foil. Bake to get the tomato juices bubbling and heat the filling, about 10 minutes. Uncover, and carefully break an egg into each indentation. Sprinkle the eggs with the remaining ⅓ cup of grated cheese and 1 teaspoon dried oregano. Bake until the egg whites are set but yolks are still a little runny, about 15 minutes.

How to Choose an Eggplant

I love cooking with seasonal vegetables, and eggplants are best through the summer into the fall. But they are available year-round, and I do buy them and cook with them all year long. This is what I look for when I buy eggplants:

I prefer small eggplants, weighing 6 to 8 ounces each. These generally have fewer and smaller seeds, which are the source of the bitterness. I try to choose eggplants of uniform width; "big-bellied" eggplants are more likely to have lots of mature seeds.

The ideal eggplant should have firm flesh, with no bruises; glossy skin, with no blemishes; and a tight skin that covers the flesh so well that it "squeaks" when you rub it. A long green stem is also an indicator that the fruit has been recently picked and is still drawing nourishment from the stem. Indeed, a fresh, vital stem, not a withered brown one, is a reassuring sign of freshness for most vegetables, as is the presence of fresh leaves on root vegetables such as carrots, beets, and turnips.

STUFFED EGGPLANT PUGLIA STYLE

Melanzane Ripiene alla Pugliese

Puglia is the region that constitutes the heel of the Italian peninsula. Seafood, a lot of vegetables, and olive oil dominate the Pugliese menu. Pugliese food is usually accompanied by some of the best semolina bread in all of Italy, made in the town of Altamura. Eggplant is popular on the Pugliese table.

Serves 6

6 small Italian eggplants (about 1½ pounds total)

⅓ cup extra-virgin olive oil

1½ teaspoons kosher salt

2 garlic cloves, peeled and chopped

2 ripe medium tomatoes, seeded and chopped

¼ teaspoon crushed red-pepper flakes

1 cup grated Grana Padano or Parmigiano-Reggiano

1 cup grated Italian Fontina

2 tablespoons chopped fresh Italian parsley

2 tablespoons chopped fresh mint

Preheat the oven to 400 degrees F. Halve the eggplants lengthwise. Scoop out any seeds, then scoop out the flesh, leaving a ½-inch shell. Cut the eggplant flesh into small cubes. In a large nonstick skillet, over medium-high heat, heat 2 tablespoons olive oil. Season the inside of the eggplant shells with 1 teaspoon of salt, then brown them, cut side down, in the oil, about 2 minutes. Remove, and place in an oiled baking dish, cut side up.

In the same skillet, heat the remaining 2 tablespoons of olive oil. Add the eggplant flesh and garlic. Once the eggplant has begun to wilt, add the tomatoes and crushed red pepper, and cook until the eggplant is tender but the tomatoes still retain their shape, about 5 minutes. Scrape the mixture into a bowl, stir in half of the grated cheeses, the parsley, and the mint. Stuff the filling into the eggplant shells, and top with the remaining grated cheeses. Cover with foil, and bake for 30 minutes. Uncover, and bake until the eggplant shells are tender and the top is browned, about 10 to 15 minutes more.

SAVORY STUFFED PEPPERS

Peperoni Ripieni

Peppers are best, as are all vegetables, when in season, but peppers are readily available most of the year, and they'll always work just fine. These peppers can be made in advance, as either an appetizer or a side dish. The recipe calls for anchovies and olives, which bring a Mediterranean flavor to the table, but, as with many of my recipes, you can make changes to the dish and omit either, and the result will still be delicious.

Serves 6

4 medium-sized red, yellow, or orange bell peppers

4 cups 1-inch day-old country-bread cubes

1 cup milk

3 tablespoons extra-virgin olive oil

2 garlic cloves, peeled and sliced

4 anchovies, chopped

2 plum tomatoes, seeded and chopped

⅓ cup pitted Gaeta olives, chopped

¼ cup drained tiny capers in brine

1 bunch scallions, chopped (about 1 cup)

1 large egg, beaten

½ cup plus 2 tablespoons grated Grana Padano or Parmigiano-Reggiano

¼ cup chopped fresh Italian parsley

¼ teaspoon kosher salt

Preheat the oven to 400 degrees F. Cut out the stems of the peppers, and cut lengthwise into thirds, to make "boats" that will hold the stuffing. Remove the pith and the seeds. Put the cubed bread in a bowl, and pour the milk over it. When the bread is softened, squeeze out the excess milk, and put the bread in a large bowl.

In a medium skillet, heat 2 tablespoons of olive oil over medium heat. When the oil is hot, add the garlic. Once the garlic is sizzling, add the anchovies, and stir to dissolve them into the oil. Add the tomatoes, olives, and capers, and cook until the tomatoes just begin to soften but still retain their shape, about 3 minutes. Add to the bowl with the bread, and let cool.

Mix the scallions, egg, grated cheese, and parsley into the bowl with the bread.

Grease a 10-by-13-inch baking dish with the remaining tablespoon olive oil. Season the inside of the peppers with the salt. Mound some stuffing into the crevice of each pepper boat, but do not overstuff; lay them, stuffing side up, in the baking dish. Cover with foil, and bake for 30 minutes. Uncover, and continue baking until the filling is browned and the peppers are tender, about 15 minutes more.

ZUCCHINI PARMIGIANA

Parmigiana di Zucchine

Zucchini is such a convenient and delicious vegetable. It is inexpensive, and you can find it year-round, although it is best in the summer. In this delicious and simple recipe, the zucchini is baked into a parmigiana but does not have the traditional frying step. I like using a large baking pan and making just one layer; this way, the zucchini will dry up more in the oven, and you will have more of the crispy cheese top, which everybody loves.

Serves 6

2 pounds medium zucchini

½ teaspoon kosher salt

1 tablespoon unsalted butter, at room temperature

4 ounces sliced whole-wheat bread

4 cups Marinara Sauce (page 80)

2 cups shredded low-moisture mozzarella

1 cup grated Grana Padano or Parmigiano-Reggiano

¼ cup chopped fresh basil

Preheat the oven to 400 degrees F. Bring a large pot of water to a boil. Add the whole zucchini, and bring back to a boil. Simmer until the zucchini are almost tender throughout, about 15 minutes. Drain, cool, and slice lengthwise into ½-inch-thick slices. Season with the salt.

Grease a 9-by-13-inch baking dish with the butter, and fit the bread in one layer into the bottom, trimming to fit if necessary.

Layer as follows: Spread the bread with 2 cups of the marinara sauce. Arrange half of the zucchini in an even layer. Sprinkle with half of the mozzarella and Grana Padano. Sprinkle with all of the basil. Arrange the remaining zucchini in an even layer. Spread with the remaining marinara, and top with the remaining mozzarella and Grana Padano. Bake, uncovered, until browned and bubbly, about 35 to 40 minutes.

EGGPLANT AND RICE PARMIGIANA

Melanzane e Riso alla Parmigiana

Everybody seems to like eggplant parmigiana, but in this recipe, a layer of cooked rice is added as the layers of eggplant are assembled. This renders the dish a bit more complex, with some starch. The beauty of a Mediterranean diet is just that, diversity. Adding a little bit of different food categories to a dish helps make the whole meal more complete. With this dish, just add a salad and you have a fully satisfying repast.

Serves 8

2 cups Arborio rice

2 fresh bay leaves

6 tablespoons extra-virgin olive oil

1¼ teaspoons kosher salt, plus more for salting the eggplant

3 Italian eggplants, cut lengthwise into ¼-inch-thick slices (about 2½ pounds before trimming)

1 cup chopped onion

6 cups canned whole San Marzano tomatoes, crushed by hand (see page 78)

½ loosely packed cup fresh basil leaves, chopped

2 cups shredded low-moisture mozzarella

1 cup grated Grana Padano or Parmigiano-Reggiano

Preheat oven to 375 degrees F. In a medium saucepan, combine the rice, 2 cups water, bay leaves, 1 tablespoon of the oil, and ¼ teaspoon of the salt. Bring to a simmer, cover, and cook until water is absorbed, about 7 minutes. The rice will still be al dente. Spread the rice onto a sheet pan to cool.

Layer the eggplant in a large colander in the sink, and sprinkle liberally with kosher salt.

Set a flat plate large enough to cover most of the eggplant slices, weighted with cans, to help press the excess liquid and bitterness from the eggplant. After about 20 minutes, rinse and drain the eggplant and pat dry.

Heat the remaining 5 tablespoons olive oil in a Dutch oven over medium heat. Add the onion and cook until softened, about 5 minutes. Add the tomatoes; slosh out the can or bowl used for crushing with 1 cup of water, and add that as well. Season with the remaining teaspoon salt, and bring to a boil. Nestle the eggplant slices in the sauce, and simmer until tender, about 15 minutes. Stir in the basil, and remove from heat.

In a medium bowl, toss together the two cheeses. Ladle about a third of the tomato sauce into a 9-by-13-inch baking dish. Fish out and layer a third of the eggplant in an overlapping pattern. Spread over that half the rice, then another third of the eggplant in overlapping slices, and a third of the sauce. Sprinkle with half the cheese. Top with the final layer of rice, then eggplant and sauce, and the last of the cheese. Cover the dish with foil, taking care not to touch the cheese, and bake until bubbly around the edges, about 25 minutes. Uncover, and bake until browned and crusty on top, another 25 to 30 minutes.

How to Freeze Dishes That
Contain Vegetables

I like my vegetables fresh and seasonal, because that is the most economical, flavorful, nutritious, and socially conscious way to shop and cook. But when I bake vegetables or prepare casseroles, it makes a lot of kitchen sense to freeze the leftovers, or even make an extra recipe and freeze it before I bake it. If by chance you have some of the Zucchini Parmigiana (page 111) or Eggplant and Rice Parmigiana (page 112) left over, cut it in portion-sized pieces, set each one snugly in a container, wrap in plastic wrap, date, and freeze it. It will keep for several weeks. To reheat the frozen dish, defrost it, and spoon on top a few tablespoons of the Marinara Sauce (page 80) that you should have in your freezer as well. Sprinkle on some grated cheese, and bake in a hot oven or toaster oven until it is hot in the inside and bubbling. Microwaving it will work just as well.

Planning and preparing ahead are the best way to have those great home-cooked meals even when you have been working all day, and these two recipes are perfect for that.

VEGGIE MEATBALLS

Polpettine di Verdure

These patties make a delicious snack, hors d'oeuvre, or sandwich stuffer. Once fried, try adding them to a bubbling tomato sauce to finish off pasta. They are traditionally fried but can be baked in a preheated 375-degree oven for 25 minutes instead. They also reheat well in the oven.

Makes 36

4 medium-small Yukon Gold potatoes, peeled (about 1¼ pounds)

3 medium zucchini, grated (about 1¼ pounds)

2 large eggs, beaten

Zest of 1 lemon, grated

½ cup breadcrumbs

½ cup grated Grana Padano or Parmigiano-Reggiano

½ cup chopped scallion

10 fresh basil leaves, chopped

2 teaspoons kosher salt, or to taste

Extra-virgin olive oil, for frying

In a medium saucepan, cook the potatoes in water to cover until tender. Drain, cool slightly, peel, and pass through a potato ricer into a large bowl. Let cool.

Put the grated zucchini in a kitchen towel, and wring out all of the excess liquid over the sink. Add the zucchini to the potatoes, along with the eggs, lemon zest, breadcrumbs, grated cheese, scallion, basil, and salt. Mix well.

Form the mixture into about thirty-six small patties. Heat a large nonstick skillet over medium-high heat. Add a film of olive oil to the pan, and cook the patties in batches until browned on both sides, about 3 minutes per side, adding more oil as needed. Drain on paper towels, and season with salt. The patties can be kept warm in a low oven while you make the next batch.

PASTAS, POLENTA, AND RISOTTOS

Pasta Wisdom

In the Italian meal courses, the course after the antipasto is all about primi—pasta, risotto, and gnocchi. The primi are served before the main course and usually follow the antipasti. Sometimes you start a meal with a primo, and sometimes the primo, a nice bowl of pasta or gnocchi, could become the main course. As far as I am concerned, a primo served with a delicious leafy salad could be lunch or even a light dinner, but I always make sure that I have a good ratio of vegetables and/or proteins in my pasta dish, to add nutritional balance.

There are two major categories of pasta for primi, fresh pasta and dried pasta. They are both equally delicious in my kitchen. Fresh pasta you can make easily at home (see page 145) or buy freshly made at your specialty store. On the other hand, dried pasta is readily available in just about any food store.

Let's focus on dried pasta, since it is such a favorite, readily available, economical, and versatile.

When buying dry pasta:

- make sure it is made from 100-percent durum wheat;
- it should be an even amber color;
- it should not be blotchy or have spots;
- it should have a matte finish, not be shiny;
- it should not be cracked.

When cooked:

- pasta should have resiliency;
- it should have a slightly nutty flavor;
- it should not stick together when cooked properly.

Boiling the Pasta

For 1 pound of pasta, bring 6 quarts of water to a full boil. Stir 1 tablespoon kosher or coarse sea salt into the boiling water before adding the pasta.

Drop shaped and tubular pasta into the boiling water, and stir immediately. For long pasta, slip it into the water and push the strands under gradually as they soften, bending them into the water, so they do not break; then slowly begin to stir to separate the strands.

After adding pasta, cover the pot but keep the cover slightly ajar, propping it open with a wooden spoon, and return water to the boil over high heat. Be prepared to uncover the pot before the water boils over.

Start timing the pasta when the boil resumes. Cook pasta at a rolling boil, following cooking-time instructions on the pasta box.

Stir the pasta occasionally. Test for doneness by extracting a piece and tasting it 1 to 2 minutes before the designated time.

Drain but do not rinse the pasta.

Corrections in Pasta Cooking

Did you forget to salt the water? Better to check before the pasta is done: sip water from a wooden spoon; it should be at least "comfortably" salty.

If you forgot to salt it, add salt right away: saltless pasta is redeemable while it's in the water, because it will absorb some salt even in a brief boil, but it's hard to correct once it is cooked and drained.

Saucing the Pasta, or, in Italian, *Condire la Pasta*

I recommend sautéing the drained pasta with the sauce before serving it. Let the two cook together a minute or two before the final seasoning and serving. The pasta will absorb some of the sauce, and the sauce will inten-

(continues)

sify in flavor. When working with dried pasta that will be finished in the skillet, cook the pasta in the water for 2 minutes less than the minimum time given on the package.

Have a big skillet ready with the sauce, and add the drained pasta. I prefer to scoop the pasta right out of the boiling water with a spider and plop it into the pan full of hot sauce. If you do not have a large enough skillet to hold all of the pasta, simply drain the pasta, always reserving a cup or two of the pasta-cooking water, return the drained pasta to the pasta-cooking pot, add just enough sauce, and bring it to a simmer. Italians do not like their pasta swimming in sauce; there should be just enough sauce to let the pasta glide—not plop—into the plate. A dish of dressed pasta should be flowing, not sticky or soupy. If it is too dry, add some of the reserved pasta-cooking water.

When pasta is properly dressed, turn off the burner and stir in grated cheeses, such as Grana Padano, Parmigiano-Reggiano, or pecorino. Cheese breaks down (the fat separates from the protein, and the cheese becomes stringy) if it is heated too long or at too high a temperature.

I prefer hot shallow bowls to flat plates for serving pasta. If you pile the pasta in the bottom of a bowl or, in the case of long shapes like spaghetti, make a little *nido* (nest), the pasta will stay hot longer.

About Saving That Pasta-Boiling Water

Pasta-cooking water is an essential component of finishing the pasta, both in the sauce-making stage and in finishing the dish. Here are tips for when to add pasta water:

- After you've caramelized all your seasonings and sauce ingredients, add pasta-cooking water from the pasta pot as a medium to extract and blend their flavors.

- Add pasta-cooking water to prevent scorching if something is browning too fast.
- In a large skillet, liquid will evaporate quickly. Replenish the moisture with pasta-cooking water whenever needed.
- If your sauce is complete but must wait awhile for the pasta to cook, it may thicken. Add some of the pasta-cooking water.
- If there's not enough sauce to coat the pasta when you're tossing them together in the skillet, add more pasta-cooking water.
- A thin pasta, like capellini or spaghetti, will absorb more liquid than a tubular pasta, so be prepared to add more water as you toss the strands with the sauce.
- Remember that the cooking water has salty and starchy qualities and adds seasoning and body during the finishing of pasta in sauce.

SPAGHETTI WITH QUICK PANTRY SAUCE

Spaghetti al Sugo della Dispensa

When you're thinking about a recipe, I am sure your thoughts immediately go to shopping and all the ingredients you are ready to buy. My advice is to try opening your cupboard. I'll bet that you will find a myriad of ingredients that will make a great pasta sauce in minutes. Now, I am thinking about an Italian cupboard, like the one I have in my home, with olives, capers, cured artichokes, sun-dried tomatoes, beans, canned tomatoes, canned tuna, and so on, but I am sure that if you search your shelves you'll find some unexpected treasures for your own sauce. Most likely, you have made sauces with some combination of the ingredients in the recipe below. The truth is, Italians have many simple pasta-sauce recipes that exist only because the ingredients were handy. This recipe falls into that category; it is convenient, economical, and full of flavor, because cured products like olives, capers, and anchovies intensify in flavor during the curing process.

Serves 6

Kosher salt for the pot, plus more if necessary

¼ cup extra-virgin olive oil

6 garlic cloves, peeled and sliced

6 anchovies, chopped

½ cup pitted coarsely chopped black brine-cured olives

¼ cup drained tiny capers in brine

One 28-ounce can whole San Marzano tomatoes, crushed by hand (see page 78)

¼ teaspoon crushed red-pepper flakes

1 pound spaghetti

¼ cup chopped fresh Italian parsley

Bring a large pot of salted water to boil for pasta. In a large skillet, heat the olive oil over medium-high heat. When the oil is hot, add the garlic. Once the garlic is sizzling, add the anchovies. Stir until the anchovies dissolve into the oil. Add the olives and capers, and let them sizzle a minute, then add the tomatoes and 1 cup only of slosh water from the can. Bring to a boil and season with the red-pepper flakes and salt if necessary, given that the ingredients are already quite salty. Continue to simmer while you cook the pasta.

Add the spaghetti to the boiling water, and cook until al dente. When the pasta is cooked, remove with tongs and add directly to the sauce. Sprinkle with the parsley, and toss to coat the pasta with the sauce. Serve hot.

I love capers, one of those ingredients that are content to stay dormant in your cupboard or refrigerator until you open the jar and then, like a genie, out the flavors come.

Capers are the unopened green flower buds of *Capparis spinosa,* a wild and cultivated crawling plant that grows in and around the Mediterranean. You can find it draping walls, rocks, and antiquities in southern Italy. The bud of the plant is harvested in the morning when it reaches the right size. The smaller the caper bud, the more precious and delicious it is. The size can range from a peppercorn to a gooseberry.

Capers generally come preserved in brine but can also be found packed in salt. Either way, it is best to rinse them before using, especially the ones packed in salt. The taste is slightly astringent, very green, and pronounced, with a nutty finish. They bring flavor to pasta sauce, fish and chicken dishes, as well as lamb and pork. If you love olives, capers are a good substitute—or a complement when they're cooked together. Try tossing some chopped capers in your burger meat next time you make patties.

A combination of capers, olive oil, garlic, and fresh lemon juice will always taste good no matter what fish or white meat you add to it.

OLIVE OIL AND ROSEMARY SPAGHETTINI

Spaghettini all'Olio e Rosmarino

This is a perfect example of a minimal-ingredient recipe that is delicious and easy. It's based on one of the primary flavors in Italian cuisine: rosemary. You will often see rosemary used in flavoring meats and roasts, because it has such an intense and rich flavor. But in this recipe, cooked in some butter to release its aroma, it makes a perfect sauce for spaghetti. Be sure to top it with some grated cheese. This is a great dish!

Serves 6

Kosher salt

1 pound spaghettini

2 tablespoons extra-virgin olive oil

3 tablespoons unsalted butter

2 bushy rosemary sprigs, needles stripped from the stems (about 3 tablespoons)

6 tablespoons chopped fresh Italian parsley

1 cup grated Grana Padano or Parmigiano-Reggiano

Bring a large pot of salted water to a boil. When you begin preparing the sauce, begin cooking the pasta.

In a large skillet, over medium-high heat, melt the butter in the olive oil. When the butter is melted, add the rosemary, and cook until the needles are sizzling and the rosemary is fragrant. Ladle in 1 cup of pasta water, and simmer to reduce by half. Stir in the parsley.

When the pasta is al dente, remove with tongs directly to the skillet. Toss to coat the pasta with the sauce. Remove the skillet from the heat, toss with the grated cheese, and serve.

VERMICELLI IN A CREAMED BROCCOLI SAUCE

Vermicelli alla Crema di Broccolo

When I see "cream" in the title of a pasta sauce I cringe, but this recipe is quite different. The cream is the puréed vegetable. It is like making pesto, but instead of basil you use blanched broccoli. And let this start your creative juices flowing: substitute for the broccoli other seasonal vegetables, or vegetables your family loves. You can also add a protein, like shrimp or chicken. This is the ultimate commonsense recipe. Just pick the right vegetable and the right protein and you're ready to go.

Serves 6

8 ounces small broccoli florets

½ cup blanched almonds, toasted

1 loosely packed cup fresh basil leaves

½ loosely packed cup fresh parsley leaves

½ teaspoon kosher salt, plus more for the pasta pot

½ cup extra-virgin olive oil

4 garlic cloves, peeled and sliced

1 pound vermicelli

1 cup grated Grana Padano or Parmigiano-Reggiano

Bring a large pot of water to a boil. Add the broccoli florets and blanch until almost tender, about 4 minutes. Save the water to cook the vermicelli. Fish the broccoli out with a spider, rinse the florets under cold water to stop the cooking process, and drain well. Put the broccoli in a food processor with the almonds, basil, parsley, and salt. Drizzle in ¼ cup of olive oil, and pulse to make a coarse purée.

In a large skillet, over medium-high heat, add 3 tablespoons of the olive oil. When the oil is hot, add the garlic. In the meantime, salt the boiling water and add the pasta. Once the garlic is sizzling, scrape in the broccoli purée. Cook and stir for a few minutes, then ladle in 1 cup of pasta water. Simmer the sauce while the pasta cooks. When the pasta is al dente, remove with tongs and add directly to the sauce. Toss to coat the pasta with the sauce. Drizzle with remaining tablespoon olive oil. Remove the skillet from the heat, stir in the grated cheese, and serve. Top with more toasted almond slivers if you like.

PIPETTE OR ELBOWS WITH SWEET POTATOES, PARSLEY, AND CAPERS

Pipette con Patate Dolci y Prezzemolo e Capperi

The combination of potatoes and pasta in one dish is not unusual in Italy. In Liguria, string beans and cubes of cooked potatoes are served on pasta, traditionally with pesto. In Naples, ditalini with peas and cubed potatoes is a standard. In this pasta recipe, instead of regular potatoes, I use sweet potatoes, which makes the recipe nutritionally more balanced. The sweetness of the potatoes is tamed by the saltiness and complexity of the capers, which makes for a delicious and nutritious plate of pasta.

Serves 6

2 tablespoons extra-virgin olive oil

4 ounces thick-sliced bacon or pancetta, cut into julienne strips

4 garlic cloves, peeled and crushed

4 fresh sage leaves

1 pound sweet potatoes, peeled, cut into ½-inch cubes

2 leeks, white and light-green parts only, sliced (about 2 cups)

¼ cup rinsed small capers (optional)

½ teaspoon kosher salt, plus more for the pot

¼ to ½ teaspoon crushed red-pepper flakes

1 pound pipette or elbow pasta

3 tablespoons chopped fresh Italian parsley

1 cup grated Grana Padano or Parmigiano-Reggiano

Bring a large pot of salted water to a boil for pasta. In a large skillet, over medium-high heat, heat the olive oil and add the bacon or pancetta, the garlic, and the sage. Cook until fat has rendered, about 3 to 4 minutes. Add the sweet potatoes and leeks, and cook, stirring continuously, until both begin to soften, about 4 minutes. Add the capers, if using. Season with the salt and crushed red pepper. Ladle in 1 cup of pasta water, and simmer rapidly until the sweet potatoes and leeks are very tender but the sweet potatoes retain their shape, about 7 to 8 minutes, adding more pasta water if necessary to keep it saucy.

Meanwhile, cook the pipette until al dente. When the pipette are done, remove with a spider directly to the sauce. Add the parsley, and toss to coat the pasta with the sauce. Increase the heat and boil a minute if the sauce is too thin, or add a little more pasta water if it is too thick. Remove the skillet from the heat, sprinkle with the grated cheese, toss, and serve.

To Prep Artichokes

The artichoke that we cook and eat is the unopened bud of the plant. In its smaller and younger form, the artichoke can be eaten almost in its entirety: leaves, heart, and stem. Once the artichoke grows, it develops a choke, which needs to be removed, and the outer leaves take on a tougher texture.

To clean an artichoke:

Fill a large bowl with a couple of quarts of cold water, and squeeze in the juice of a medium-sized lemon (drop in the cut lemon halves, too). This acidulated-water bath will minimize the discoloration of peeled artichokes caused by oxidation.

Trim one artichoke at a time. First snap off the thick outside leaves until you reach the tender, pale inner leaves.

With a sharp paring knife or vegetable peeler, shave off the dark skin of the stem, exposing the tender core. Peel around the globe of the artichoke, too, removing the dark-green spots where the tough leaves were attached.

Cut across the leaf tips with a serrated knife, removing the tough top third of the artichoke. Slice the entire artichoke in half lengthwise, splitting the bulb and stem. Scrape out the choke (found in mature artichokes) with a paring knife or the edge of a teaspoon, and discard. Drop the cleaned pieces into the acidulated water.

To prep artichokes for Artichoke Carbonara (page 130), thinly slice each cleaned artichoke half lengthwise, and drop slices back into acidulated water as you cut them. Drain them well when ready to add them to the pot.

ARTICHOKE CARBONARA
Carbonara di Carciofi

In spaghetti-carbonara recipes, egg yolks always appear in the ingredients list; they bind the ingredients and give a finished shine to the dish. Although I think the addition of the egg in the traditional carbonara was to add a nutritional element for the hardworking miners and land workers, today it serves more as an enhancer of flavor and texture for the dish.

Serves 6

¾ teaspoon kosher salt, plus more
   for the pot

1 pound penne

¼ cup extra-virgin olive oil

2 large or 3 small artichokes, prepped
   and thinly sliced (see page 129)

1 cup frozen peas, thawed

¼ teaspoon crushed red-pepper
   flakes

4 large eggs

1 cup grated Grana Padano or
   Parmigiano-Reggiano

1 cup heavy cream

2 tablespoons butter for the pan

Preheat the oven to 375 degrees F. Bring a large pot of salted water to a boil for pasta. Add the penne, and cook until al dente.

Meanwhile, in an 11- or 12-inch cast-iron (or nonstick) skillet, heat the olive oil over medium-high heat. Add the artichokes, and cook until they begin to soften, about 5 minutes. Add the peas, and ladle in 1 cup of pasta water. Season with ½ teaspoon salt and the red-pepper flakes, cover, and simmer until vegetables are very tender, about 5 minutes more. Uncover, and raise the heat to cook away any excess liquid; there should be just enough liquid to coat the bottom of the pan.

While the vegetables cook, whisk together the eggs, ¼ cup of the grated cheese, the cream, and the remaining ¼ teaspoon salt in a medium bowl. Butter a medium-sized baking pan.

When the vegetables and pasta are ready, scoop the pasta into the skillet with a spider, and toss to combine. Remove from heat, and let cool for a minute; then stir in the egg, cheese, and cream mixture. Set all in the buttered baking dish. Sprinkle with the remaining ¾ cup grated cheese, and bake until set and crusty, about 20 minutes. Cool for a few minutes before serving.

FETTUCCINE WITH A CLAM AND LEEK SAUCE

Fettuccine alle Vongole e Porri

Clams and pasta are a marriage made in Italian heaven. Here is a different version from the traditional garlic and oil. It is especially good for people who have a hard time digesting garlic, because the garlic is sliced and can be removed after cooking. Do not forfeit the flavor of garlic in your cooking, however; crush the cloves, remembering how many you put in, and then fish them out.

Dry or fresh fettuccine would both be delicious for this recipe; just keep in mind the different cooking times of the two pastas.

Serves 6

½ teaspoon kosher salt, plus more for the pot

24 littleneck clams, scrubbed

6 tablespoons extra-virgin olive oil

6 garlic cloves, peeled and sliced

2 leeks, halved lengthwise, white and light-green parts thinly sliced

12 ounces zucchini, sliced into ¼-inch-thick half-moons

1 pound dry fettuccine or fresh (page 145)

¼ teaspoon crushed red-pepper flakes

2 cups San Marzano canned whole tomatoes, crushed by hand (see page 78)

¼ loosely packed cup fresh basil leaves, chopped

Bring a large pot of salted water to a boil for pasta. Shuck the clams, reserving shucking juices. Strain the juices. Roughly chop the clam meat.

In a large skillet, over medium-high heat, heat 4 tablespoons of the olive oil. When the oil is hot, add the garlic. Once the garlic is sizzling, add the leeks and zucchini. Cook until softened, about 4 minutes. Once you start cooking the vegetables, begin to cook the pasta.

Season the vegetables with the salt and crushed red pepper. Add the tomatoes, the reserved clam juices, and ½ cup water. Bring to a simmer, and cook until slightly thickened, about 4 minutes.

When the pasta is al dente, drain and add to the sauce, along with the chopped clams. Add the basil, and toss to coat the pasta with the sauce. Remove the skillet from the heat, drizzle with the remaining 2 tablespoons oil, toss, and serve hot.

DITALINI WITH LENTILS AND SHRIMP
Ditalini Mare e Monti

Lentils are one of my favorite legumes: delicious, readily available, economical, and a nutritional powerhouse. Lentils are delicious by themselves, or with vegetables, fish, or meat. This dish has the elements to make a complete meal—pasta, legumes, and shrimp. Just be sure not to overcook the shrimp, and to add the cooked ditalini just before serving, or the pasta will become mushy.

Serves 6

2 cups of ditalini

6 tablespoons extra-virgin olive oil

1 cup chopped onion

6 garlic cloves, peeled and crushed

1 cup peeled, chopped carrot

1 cup chopped celery

1 teaspoon kosher salt

One 28-ounce can whole San Marzano tomatoes, crushed by hand (see page 78)

8 ounces dried lentils, rinsed and drained

1 pound medium shrimp, peeled and deveined

2 tablespoons chopped fresh Italian parsley

Cook the ditalini in salted water, leaving it al dente. Drain and reserve the cooking water to add to the lentils.

In a large soup pot, over medium heat, heat 4 tablespoons of the olive oil. Once the oil is hot, add the onion and garlic. Cook until the onion begins to soften, about 3 to 4 minutes. Add the carrot and celery, and cook until softened, about 5 minutes.

Season with the salt, and add the tomatoes and 6 cups of water. Cover, bring to a simmer, and cook until slightly thickened and flavorful, about 30 minutes.

Add the lentils, and continue simmering until they are tender, about 30 minutes. (You may need to add another cup or so of water, if the pan seems dry and the lentils are not getting tender.)

When the lentils are done, stir in the shrimp, and simmer until they are just cooked through, only 2 or 3 minutes. Stir in the cooked ditalini, the remaining 2 tablespoons olive oil, and the chopped parsley, bring all to a boil, and serve.

PENNE WITH RICOTTA AND MUSHROOMS
Penne Ricotta e Funghi

This is a simple recipe, packed with flavor and with a great mouth texture. It can also be made in any season of the year, since mushrooms now abound on our store shelves year-round. I love mushrooms; they deliver a lot of flavor and texture without the heavy calories. The creaminess of the ricotta adds to the complexity of flavor, and the pasta carries it all deliciously.

Serves 6

1 teaspoon kosher salt, plus more for the pot

¼ cup extra-virgin olive oil

6 garlic cloves, peeled and sliced

1 teaspoon chopped fresh rosemary needles

1 pound mixed fresh mushrooms (button, cremini, shiitake, chanterelles)

1 bunch scallions, trimmed and chopped

1 pound penne

1½ cups of fresh ricotta (about 12 ounces)

¼ cup chopped fresh Italian parsley

½ cup grated Grana Padano or Parmigiano-Reggiano

Bring a large pot of salted water to a boil for pasta. In a large skillet, over medium heat, heat the olive oil. When the oil is hot, add the garlic, and cook until it is sizzling. Add the rosemary, and cook a few seconds, until fragrant. Raise the heat to medium-high, add the mushrooms, and season with the salt. Cook until the mushrooms are browned and wilted, about 3 minutes. Add the scallions, and cook until wilted, about 2 minutes. Ladle in 1 cup pasta water, and simmer until mushrooms are tender, about 10 minutes.

While the sauce simmers, cook the pasta. When the sauce is ready and the pasta is al dente, remove the penne with a spider and add it directly to the sauce. Stir in the ricotta and parsley, and cook until warmed through. Remove the skillet from the heat, stir in the grated cheese, and serve.

MAFALDE WITH RICOTTA AND MEAT RAGÙ

Mafalde al Ragù con la Ricotta

Ricotta is used a lot in Italian pasta dishes. My guess is that the herdsmen did not always have aged cheese to grate, whereas ricotta could be, and most likely was, made every morning. So, when it came to lunch or dinner, a dollop of fresh ricotta in the cooked pasta always did the trick. Ricotta that we have available in the stores is mostly made from cow's milk, but ricotta is also made from sheep's milk or goat's milk. If you have an opportunity, try to get the other varieties; they reflect the unique flavors of the different milks and will impart those flavors to your pasta. Ricotta is usually made from the whey after cheese has been made, so it is lower in fat than hard cheese. It keeps in the refrigerator, covered with plastic wrap, for 3 or 4 days.

Serves 6

1 teaspoon kosher salt, plus more for the pot

3 tablespoons extra-virgin olive oil

12 ounces sweet Italian sausage, removed from casing

3 garlic cloves, peeled and crushed

1 medium onion, sliced

½ teaspoon crushed red-pepper flakes

One 28-ounce can whole San Marzano tomatoes, crushed by hand (see page 78)

1 pound mafalde or fettuccine

1 cup drained fresh ricotta

½ cup grated Grana Padano or Parmigiano-Reggiano

Bring a large pot of salted water to a boil for pasta. In a large skillet, over medium heat, heat the olive oil. When the oil is hot, add the sausage and garlic, and cook until the sausage is browned, breaking it up with a wooden spoon as you go, about 3 or 4 minutes. Add the sliced onion, and season with the salt and the red-pepper flakes. Cook until onion is wilted, about 5 minutes.

Add the tomatoes, slosh the tomato can out with 1 cup water, and add that as well. Bring to a simmer, and cook until thick and flavorful, about 20 minutes.

Meanwhile, cook the pasta in the boiling water. When the pasta is al dente, transfer it to the finished sauce, picking it out of the boiling water with tongs, letting the excess water drip back into the boiling pot. Toss to coat the pasta with the sauce. Remove the skillet from the heat, stir in the ricotta and grated cheese, and serve.

MAFALDE FLORENTINE STYLE

Mafalde alla Fiorentina

Once, during my many years researching Italian recipes, I found a spinach dish that was attributed to Michelangelo. It contained raisins and pignoli along with the braised spinach. It seemed natural for me to build upon those basic pedigree ingredients and make this delicious pasta dish.

Serves 6

½ teaspoon kosher salt, plus more
  for the pot

¼ cup golden raisins

2 tablespoons extra-virgin olive oil

¼ cup pine nuts

One 5-ounce bag fresh spinach,
  chopped

1 pound mafalde or fettuccine

Pinch freshly grated nutmeg

1½ cups drained fresh ricotta

½ cup grated Grana Padano or
  Parmigiano-Reggiano

Bring a large pot of salted water to a boil for pasta. Soak the raisins in hot water to cover for 10 minutes, then drain.

In a large skillet, heat the olive oil over medium heat. Add the pine nuts, and cook, stirring, until toasted, about 2 minutes. Add the spinach, and season with the salt. Once the spinach is in the skillet, start cooking the pasta.

Let the spinach cook until wilted, about 3 or 4 minutes, then ladle in 1 cup pasta water and add the raisins and nutmeg. Simmer until the pasta is ready. Once the pasta is almost done, stir the ricotta into the sauce over low heat. Remove the pasta with tongs, and add directly to the sauce, adding a little more pasta water if the pasta seems dry. Remove the skillet from the heat, stir in the grated cheese, and serve.

Different shapes of pasta work best when paired with specific sauces. The smoothness or the number of ridges, the nooks and crannies, the thickness or thinness capture and absorb sauce in different ways and provide a pleasing play of texture with the components of the sauce.

Long, dried pasta, such as capellini, spaghetti, or linguine, marry best with olive-oil-based sauces, because the oil coats the pasta completely without drowning it. Flavors that go well with oil-based sauces are fish, vegetables, and puréed herbs. It is important to bear in mind how you cut up the ingredients for the sauce. For long pasta, the vegetables, fish, or meat should be cut stringlike rather than cubed, so they can blend better with the pasta and sauce when eaten.

Short, tubular pasta goes especially well with sauces that are chunky, so cut the vegetables, fish, or meat for the sauce into small pieces, cubed; in this scenario, the pieces of meat, vegetable, or beans in the sauce are captured in the crevices of the pasta. Sauces made with ricotta cheese, olives, or mozzarella also go very well with the short, dry pasta. Short, particularly tubular, pasta is also better for oven-baked preparations.

Tomato and simple cream and butter sauces are universal and will go well with basically any pasta shape—fresh or dried.

Whatever the sauce, the pasta should be lubricated but not suffocated by it. Pasta should be thoroughly coated without lying in pools of sauce; it should glide on the plate when touched with a fork without becoming glued together.

BAKED WHOLE WHEAT PENNE
WITH CHICKPEAS

Timballo di Penne Integrali con Crema di Ceci

Whole-wheat pasta is a great alternative to regular pasta, and in the Italian tradition it is not a novelty. In Italy, pastas are made from buckwheat, farro, corn, chestnut, and chickpea flour, just to name a few. What is important to know is that each flour dictates a different cooking time for the pasta. For whole wheat, make sure to follow the instructions on cooking time; it does take longer than regular pasta, because the bran part has to be cooked. If it is not cooked enough, it remains chewy and won't absorb the sauce well.

Serves 8

2 cups dry chickpeas, soaked overnight and drained

4 fresh bay leaves

½ teaspoon kosher salt, plus more for the pot

3 tablespoons extra-virgin olive oil

4 garlic cloves, peeled and sliced

¼ teaspoon crushed red-pepper flakes

One 15-ounce can whole San Marzano tomatoes, crushed by hand (see page 78)

4 fresh sage leaves

1 pound whole-wheat penne

2 cups grated Grana Padano or Parmigiano-Reggiano

Unsalted butter, for the baking dish

2 cups shredded low-moisture mozzarella

Combine the drained chickpeas, bay leaves, and 2 quarts water. Bring to a simmer, and cook until tender, about 1 hour. Drain, and discard the bay leaves.

Preheat the oven to 350 degrees F. Bring a large pot of salted water to a boil for pasta. In a large skillet, heat the olive oil over medium-high heat. Add the garlic. Once the garlic is sizzling, add the red-pepper flakes and tomatoes, along with 1 cup of slosh water from the tomato can. Add the sage, salt, and cooked chickpeas. Bring to a simmer, and cook until thickened, about 10 minutes.

While the sauce simmers, cook the pasta until it is al dente. Transfer the pasta with a spider to the sauce, and add 1 cup pasta water. Simmer until the sauce just comes together again, about 1 minute. Remove the skillet from the heat, and stir in 1 cup grated Grana Padano or Parmigiano-Reggiano.

Grease a 4-quart baking dish with butter, and pour in the pasta-and-sauce mixture. In a small bowl, toss together the remaining Grana Padano or Parmigiano-Reggiano and the shredded mozzarella, and sprinkle over the pasta. Bake until the cheese is bubbly and golden, about 30 minutes. Serve.

BAKED DITALINI

Budino di Ditalini

Ditale in Italian means "thimble," and hence the name of this delightful little tubular pasta. *It is great in soups, but even better when baked. This dish is like a pasta pudding—a savory dish with all the luxury of dessert.*

Serves 6

1 tablespoon unsalted butter, at room temperature

2 tablespoons dried breadcrumbs

½ teaspoon kosher salt, plus more for the pot

1 pound ditalini

4 large eggs

1 cup heavy cream

1 cup milk

2 cups frozen peas, thawed and drained

1½ cups grated Grana Padano or Parmigiano-Reggiano

Preheat the oven to 350 degrees F. Butter a 4-quart rectangular baking dish, and coat with the breadcrumbs, tapping out any excess.

Bring a large pot of salted water to a boil, add the ditalini, and cook until al dente. Drain and rinse, let cool, and shake dry.

In a large bowl, whisk together the eggs and salt. Add the cream and milk slowly, and whisk until smooth. Stir in the pasta, peas, and 1 cup of the grated cheese. Spread the mixture into the prepared baking dish, and sprinkle with the remaining ½ cup of grated cheese. Bake until the custard is set, about 40 minutes. Let rest about 10 minutes before serving.

BAKED RIGATONI AND ZUCCHINI

Timballo di Rigatoni e Zucchine

Zucchini is best in the summer, which is when this dish really excels. Today one can get zucchini at a reasonable price year-round, so it's easy to make this dish for the family at any time of the year. To balance it further, add some protein, such as swordfish, shrimp, crumbled sausages, or shredded chicken breast. You can add as little or as much of each ingredient to this recipe as you want, to satisfy your nutritional preferences and, of course, your taste.

Serves 6 to 8

½ teaspoon kosher salt, plus more
  for the pot

¼ cup extra-virgin olive oil

1 medium onion, sliced

1 pound medium zucchini, sliced

One 28-ounce can whole San Marzano tomatoes, crushed by hand
  (see page 78)

1 loosely packed cup fresh basil
  leaves, roughly chopped

1 pound rigatoni

1 tablespoon unsalted butter

8 ounces shredded Fontina

1 cup grated Grana Padano or
  Parmigiano-Reggiano

Preheat the oven to 400 degrees F. Bring a large pot of salted water to a boil for pasta. In a large skillet, heat the olive oil over medium heat. Add the onion, and cook until it begins to soften, about 5 minutes. Add the zucchini, and cook until it begins to soften, another 5 minutes. Add the salt then the crushed tomatoes, slosh the tomato can out with 1 cup water, and add it to the skillet as well. Bring the sauce to a boil, and simmer just until it thickens, about 8 to 10 minutes, but don't let the zucchini begin to fall apart. Then toss in the chopped basil.

Meanwhile, cook the rigatoni until al dente, a few minutes shy of the package directions. Drain the pasta, and toss it in the skillet with the tomato sauce and basil. Butter a 9-by-13-inch baking dish. In a medium bowl, toss together the two cheeses. Spread half the pasta and sauce in the baking dish, and top with half the cheese. Layer the remaining pasta and sauce, then the remaining cheese. Bake, uncovered, until browned and bubbly, about 20 minutes.

FRESH PASTA

Pasta Fresca

Everybody likes fresh pasta, but people believe it is difficult to make. Today, with a food processor and a small hand pasta-roller, it is a cinch, as well as a great project for the whole family, no matter what age.

There are many recipes for fresh pasta, but this simple, straightforward one always works for me. Use it for any recipe calling for fresh pasta, such as the Pappardelle with Turkey Rolls (page 215).

Makes 1 pound

2 cups all-purpose flour, plus more
  for rolling

2 large eggs, beaten

½ teaspoon salt

¼ cup extra-virgin olive oil

3 tablespoons cold water

Put the flour in a food processor, and pulse a few times to aerate. In a spouted measuring cup, beat together the eggs, salt, oil, and water. With the machine running, pour in the egg mixture; let it run for about 10 seconds. Take a look to see if the dough is coming together. If it's still crumbly, sprinkle in a few teaspoons of water and process. If it's very wet and sticky, add another tablespoon of flour, and process again.

Once the consistency seems right, process the dough until it forms a ball around the blade, about 20 or 30 seconds. Dump the dough onto a floured counter, and knead a few times to smooth the dough texture. The dough should be silky and soft but not sticky; it should spring back when pressed. Wrap the dough in plastic, and let it rest at least 30 minutes before rolling.

TO ROLL PASTA SHEETS TO MAKE PAPPARDELLE, FETTUCCINE, OR RAVIOLI

Pasta can be rolled by hand (cut into four pieces and roll thin with a rolling pin) or by machine, per the instructions below:

Cut the dough into four pieces, keeping the remaining pieces wrapped as you roll the others. Sprinkle two sheet pans with flour.

Flour a dough piece and the machine rollers, and set the machine on the widest setting. Press the dough into a rectangle, fold it in half, and roll it through. Fold the dough into thirds, like a letter, and roll through with the fold on one

(recipe continues)

side. Repeat the folding and rolling at least three or four more times. Then set that piece aside, and roll the other three pieces in the same fashion. Keep the rolled pieces floured and covered with a kitchen towel.

Skip the machine to the third setting, and roll one piece through, short end first. Repeat once more, then repeat the whole process with the other three strips, keeping them covered and floured while you are rolling the other pieces.

Skip to the fifth setting, and do exactly as you did on the third setting. If the pasta strips are getting too long (more than 24 inches), halve them crosswise.

Depending on your pasta machine, you may want to stop here. You should be just able to see your hand beneath the dough if it's thin enough. If not, go to the next setting and roll once more.

To cut the pasta, you can send it through the cutting attachment on your machine, or cut by hand.

To cut by hand, lay a strip on the counter with the long side facing you. Fold in thirds the long way, like a letter, then fold in half the long way again, to make a thin strip. Cut through the strip to make your desired pasta shape—for example, cut at 1½-inch intervals for pappardelle, smaller for fettuccine. Unravel cut pasta, dust with flour, and pile to make loose nests. Set on floured sheet pans.

TO MAKE RAVIOLI

For the filling use the recipe on page 152, omitting the ½ cup of all-purpose flour.

To fill and shape the ravioli: Cut the pasta dough into four pieces, and roll them all through the pasta machine at progressively narrower settings into sheets six inches wide, or as wide as your machine allows. Lay one sheet of dough on a lightly floured surface with the long edge running left to right in front of you. Drop rounded tablespoons of filling every three inches, from left to right, on the bottom half of the pasta sheet. With a pastry brush dipped in water, moisten the edges of the sheet and the dough in between the mounds of filling, to help the dough stick together. Now fold the top of the sheet over the filling, so the top edge aligns with the bottom. Press the dough lightly, so it adheres and encloses each mound of filling. Run the pastry cutter in between the mounds, creating 2½-to-3-inch square ravioli. Press the edges of the squares, to make sure the pasta has sealed. Set the ravioli on a lightly floured tray. Fill all the remaining rolled sheets of pasta in the same way.

To cook the ravioli, bring 8 quarts water with 2 tablespoons of salt to a boil in a wide pot. Pour Marinara Sauce (page 80) into one or two skillets, depending on the amount of ravioli you're making. Have the sauce already simmering while you cook the ravioli. Drop the ravioli into the boiling water, and return it to a boil. Cook for 3 to 4 minutes, gently stirring and turning the ravioli to keep them from sticking. When they're cooked through, lift them from the pot with a spider, drain off excess water, and slide them into the sauce. Spread the ravioli in one layer in the skillet, spooning the hot sauce over them and shaking the pan to coat them thoroughly. When they're well coated and bubbling, remove the pan from the heat, sprinkle grated cheese over the ravioli if you like, and arrange on warm plates, spooning any remaining hot sauce from the skillet over the plated ravioli.

MEATBALL AND EGGPLANT TAGLIATELLE

Tagliatelle con Polpette e Melanzane

Pasta is such a popular dish, and yet we all worry about eating too much starch. Well, the answer is to balance the carbohydrates with meat and vegetables, as in this recipe. When you do, there is no compromise in flavor or satisfaction. For that Sunday-meal feeling and taste, use the fresh fettuccine recipe on page 145. This recipe makes enough sauce to freeze some for another meal.

Makes 3 quarts, enough for
3 pounds of pasta

MEATBALLS

1 pound ground chuck

½ cup finely chopped onion

½ cup grated Grana Padano

½ cup fine dried breadcrumbs

1 large egg, beaten

2 tablespoons chopped fresh parsley

1 teaspoon kosher salt

SAUCE AND PASTA

¼ cup extra-virgin olive oil

6 garlic cloves, peeled and sliced

1 medium Italian eggplant, peeled, cut into ½-inch cubes

Two 28-ounce cans whole San Marzano tomatoes, crushed by hand (see page 78)

Kosher salt for the pot

1 pound tagliatelle

¼ loosely packed cup fresh basil leaves, chopped

½ cup grated Grana Padano

For the meatballs: Combine all of the listed ingredients in a large bowl, and mix well. Form into 1½-inch meatballs and place on a sheet pan.

For the sauce: In a large straight-sided skillet, heat the olive oil over medium heat. When the oil is hot, add the garlic. Once the garlic is sizzling, add the eggplant. Brown the eggplant on all sides, about 3 to 4 minutes on each side, then add the tomatoes. Slosh out the cans with 2 cups pasta water, and add it to the skillet. Bring the sauce to a simmer, and cook until eggplant is almost tender, about 10 to 15 minutes. Add the meatballs (raw), and continue simmering until the meat is cooked through, about 20 minutes more.

In the meantime, bring to a boil a large pot of salted water to cook the pasta. While the pasta cooks, transfer half of the meatballs and sauce to a container, to freeze or refrigerate for another time, leaving half of the sauce and meatballs simmering in the skillet. When the pasta is al dente, transfer it to the sauce with tongs, and sprinkle with the basil. Toss to coat the pasta with the sauce, adding a little pasta water if the sauce seems too thick. Remove the skillet from the heat, toss in the grated cheese, and serve.

QUICK TIP

To make a serving for six, use half of the sauce and meatballs with 1 pound of dry or fresh fettuccine. Don't forget the fresh basil and grated Grana Padano!

SHELLS WITH CHICKEN SAUCE

Conchiglie al Sugo di Pollo

We all love pasta but try not to eat too much of it; healthy eating is always a question of balance. In this recipe, the pasta is dressed with proteins. Eating delicious pasta while simultaneously increasing the proportion of healthy protein is the way to go. Feel comfortable about substituting different-grain pasta; buckwheat, whole wheat, barley, and others all work well in this or any other pasta recipe. If you have time to make fresh pasta, fresh fettuccine would be delicious with this sauce.

Serves 6

1 teaspoon kosher salt, plus more for the pot

¼ cup extra-virgin olive oil

1 pound medium zucchini (about 3 zucchini), cut into ¼-inch rounds

1 pound boneless, skinless chicken breast, cut into 2-by-½-inch strips

2 garlic cloves, peeled and sliced

One 28-ounce can whole San Marzano tomatoes, crushed by hand (see page 78)

2 fresh bay leaves

Pinch crushed red-pepper flakes

1 pound medium shell pasta, or 1 pound of fresh fettucine (page 145)

1 bunch scallions, trimmed and chopped (about 1 cup)

⅓ cup grated Grana Padano or Parmigiano-Reggiano

Bring a large pot of salted water to a boil for pasta. In a large Dutch oven, heat 3 tablespoons of the oil over medium-high heat. Add the zucchini, and brown on both sides, about 2 to 3 minutes in all. Remove to a plate, add the chicken to the Dutch oven, and sear all over, another 2 to 3 minutes. Remove to the plate with the zucchini.

Add the remaining tablespoon of olive oil to the pot, along with the garlic. Once the garlic is sizzling, add the tomatoes and bay leaves, slosh the can out with 1 cup pasta water, and add that as well. Season with the salt and the crushed red-pepper flakes. Bring to a simmer, uncovered, while you cook the shells.

After the sauce has simmered 5 minutes, put the chicken and zucchini back in the pot. Drain the shells while still al dente, or remove with a spider, and add directly to the simmering sauce. Stir in the scallions, and cook until wilted, about 1 minute. Toss to coat the pasta with the sauce. Remove the Dutch oven from the heat, stir in the grated cheese, and serve.

PENNE WITH A CABBAGE AND MEAT SAUCE

Penne alla Bisnonna

This is a great seasonal pasta sauce. It makes nutritional sense, is full of flavor, and is economical, especially for large families. And as I always say, you can change the proportion of vegetables, meats, and pasta. Again, this is a commonsense decision: if you want, you can substitute chicken or chopped turkey for the sausages. Whatever you choose, you need to cook the ingredients slowly for a while, until the cabbage becomes mellow and sweet. Penne is delicious with this recipe, but for a special occasion you can serve this sauce with fresh pappardelle.

Serves 6

Kosher salt

6 tablespoons extra-virgin olive oil

½ pound sweet Italian sausage, removed from the casing

½ cup peeled, chopped carrot

½ cup chopped onion

½ cup chopped celery

¼ teaspoon crushed red-pepper flakes

2 tablespoons tomato paste

½ head Savoy cabbage, cored and shredded (about 4 cups)

1 pound penne, or 1 pound fresh pappardelle (page 145)

½ cup grated Grana Padano or Parmigiano-Reggiano

Bring a large pot of salted water to a boil for pasta. To a large, deep skillet, over medium-high heat, add 4 tablespoons of the olive oil. When the oil is hot, add the sausage. Cook, crumbling with a wooden spoon, until browned, about 3 minutes.

Add the carrot, onion, and celery, and cook until softened, about 5 minutes. Season with the red-pepper flakes. Make an empty spot in the pan, add the tomato paste, and let it toast for a minute or two. Stir the tomato paste into the vegetables, then add the cabbage and 3 cups pasta water. Cover, and cook until the cabbage is wilted, about 20 minutes. Uncover, and continue cooking to thicken the sauce and until the cabbage is tender, about 10 minutes.

Meanwhile, cook the penne until al dente. Drain the pasta, and add to the sauce. Drizzle with the remaining 2 tablespoons olive oil, and toss to coat the pasta with the sauce. Remove the skillet from the heat, add the grated cheese, toss, and serve.

RAVIOLI FILLING

Ravioli Verdi

This dish is just ravioli filling, without the pasta. (See page 145 for the pasta recipe and how to finish it.) What is important in this recipe is the ratio of the wet ingredients to the dry ingredients. Even though I give you precise measurements, the ingredients themselves vary and affect the outcome of the recipe. This is something you need to keep in mind whenever following a recipe. Use your experience and common sense to deal with any variations that might arise. In this recipe, for instance, the balls of filling must feel good and solid before you decide exactly when or if you need to add more flour. As an extra precaution, do a test by plopping one of them into the boiling water to see how they fare; it should remain whole, although a few crumbs of filling will detach in the boiling water. If it falls apart, you need a little more flour.

Serves 6

½ teaspoon kosher salt, plus more for the pot

2 bunches Swiss chard (about 2 pounds)

1 pound fresh ricotta, drained several hours or overnight

3 large eggs, beaten

1½ cups grated Grana Padano or Parmigiano-Reggiano

½ cup all-purpose flour, plus more for rolling

4 tablespoons unsalted butter

Bring a large pot of salted water to boil. Wash the chard, and remove the stems and center rib (if tough). Shred the chard. Blanch until tender, about 5 minutes. Drain, cool, and squeeze very dry. Finely chop the chard. Heat a new, clean pot of salted water, and bring to a simmer for the ravioli.

In a large bowl, stir together the ricotta, eggs, 1 cup grated cheese, the ½ cup flour, the salt, and the chard. Spread about a cup of flour on a rimmed sheet pan. Roll the dough into walnut-sized balls, then dust lightly in the flour.

Melt the butter in a large skillet over low heat. Drop the balls into the simmering water, cooking in batches if necessary, until they rise to the surface and are firm to the touch, about 5 minutes per batch. Remove with a spider or slotted spoon, letting the excess water drain off, and place them directly into the skillet with melted butter. Once all of the ravioli are in the skillet, turn off the heat and gently toss with the butter and remaining ½ cup grated cheese. Fill, shape, and cook ravioli as in procedure in preceding recipe.

CHEESE GNOCCHI
Gnocchi di Formaggio

I love potato gnocchi, but these ricotta gnocchi are a close second. They are quicker to make, there are no potatoes to cook, and for starch-conscious eaters this is a sensible gnocchi meal. Here the sauce is just the cheese, but you can drizzle on some tomato sauce or pesto if you like.

Serves 6

FOR THE GNOCCHI

Kosher salt, for the pot

1½ pounds fresh ricotta, drained

2 cups grated Grana Padano or
  Parmigiano-Reggiano

¾ cup all-purpose flour, plus more
  for rolling the gnocchi

4 large egg yolks

2 tablespoons chopped parsley

Pinch freshly ground white pepper

Pinch freshly grated nutmeg

FOR FINISHING THE GNOCCHI

4 tablespoons unsalted butter

8 whole fresh sage leaves

¼ cup freshly grated Grana Padano
  or Parmigiano-Reggiano

Bring a large, wide pot of salted water to a boil to cook the gnocchi. In a large bowl, mix all of the ingredients for the gnocchi to make a smooth dough.

Heat a large, wide skillet over medium heat. Melt the butter. When the butter is melted, add the sage. Let the sage sizzle a few minutes to flavor the butter, then keep sauce warm while you make the gnocchi.

To make the gnocchi: Spread some flour on a rimmed baking sheet or plate. Dust your hands with flour, and on a smooth surface roll the dough into ½-inch by 2-inch-long logs. Cut the log into ½-inch gnocchi, flour, and shape them by rolling on a gnocchi board. Drop the gnocchi into the flour, and dust lightly.

Cook the gnocchi in simmering water until cooked through (you will have to do this in batches—don't crowd the pot), about 2 to 3 minutes of simmering after they float to the surface. Remove gnocchi with a slotted spoon or spider, and gently add to the sage butter. Let them sit undisturbed while you cook the remaining gnocchi. Once all of the gnocchi are in the pan, let them sit for a couple minutes to firm up, then reheat over low heat, to coat the gnocchi in the sage butter. Remove the skillet from the heat, sprinkle with the grated cheese, and serve.

> **QUICK TIP**
> One can shape gnocchi by rolling them on the tines of a fork but the gnocchi board, a small handheld ridged wooden board, is much easier. It is found in most kitchen supply stores and it is inexpensive, a nice tool to have in your kitchen.

Polenta Wisdom

Polenta is the Italian version of grits. Corn came to Italy from the New World, and quickly took root. In northeastern Italy, it is the starch staple of choice, beating out pasta. It can be cooked plain, or you can add vegetables or cheese to it while cooking. The beauty of polenta is not only its flavor but also its texture, and once it's cooked you can eat it flowing and piping hot or let it cool and solidify. You can then bake it, fry it, or grill it.

To chill polenta: Pour the polenta, either freshly made or leftover, into a baking pan to a thickness of about ½ inch. Pat it flat with a rubber spatula. Cover with plastic wrap applied directly to the surface, and refrigerate until thoroughly chilled and very firm, 4 to 5 hours. Once it's firm, invert the polenta onto a cutting board, and cut into any desired shape for grilling, baking, or frying.

To bake the polenta: Place pieces on a lightly oiled baking sheet, and place in a preheated 375-degree oven until lightly browned and crispy, about 20 minutes. Turn the polenta once, about halfway through the cooking. For more flavor sprinkle the pieces of polenta with grated cheese.

To grill polenta: Lightly brush with olive oil both sides of the polenta pieces you have cut from chilled polenta. Place on a hot grill, and cook, turning once, until well marked and heated through, about 2 minutes per side.

To pan-fry polenta: Heat a small amount of olive oil in a nonstick skillet over medium-high heat. Add the polenta slices, and cook, turning once, until golden brown and crispy on both sides, 8 to 10 minutes.

Here are some serving suggestions:

Bake in the oven polenta layered with Braised Cabbage with Prosciutto (page 100), or Cabbage and Meat Sauce (page 151), topped with shredded Fontina cheese.

Serve grilled polenta with Gluttonous Tomatoes (page 106).

Top fried polenta with Marinara Sauce (page 80), and sprinkle with grated Grana Padano.

Sauté some shrimp with garlic and oil, add a cup or two of Marinara Sauce (page 80), and place this on top of a mound of polenta.

Try some of the sauce from Meatball and Eggplant Tagliatelle (page 148) on hot soft polenta or grilled polenta.

Next day, for breakfast, heat up some milk with some raisins almost to the boiling point. Cut some leftover polenta into cubes, and add them to the hot milk; sweeten to your taste with honey. This is a great way to begin the day; it was and still is one of my favorite breakfasts.

POLENTA WITH SARDINES OR ANCHOVIES

Polenta e Alici

Polenta with a little fish was one of the mainstays in the diet of the poor in northern Italy. I have talked to Piemontesi who recall passing salted anchovies around the table and dipping them in the firm polenta, to flavor it and make them last longer.

In Vicenza, on the other hand, they used salted or smoked herring, and chopped it up. A little went a long way. Here I give you two options—sardines or anchovies—both delicious. Sardines and anchovies are packed with flavor, and a little goes a long way.

Serves 6 to 8

POLENTA

1 tablespoon extra-virgin olive oil

1 tablespoon kosher salt

2 cups polenta

1 cup chopped scallions

SARDINES

Two 3¾-ounce tins skinless, boneless sardines in oil, drained

¼ cup extra-virgin olive oil

Juice of 1 lemon

3 tablespoons chopped fresh Italian parsley

¼ teaspoon crushed red-pepper flakes

ANCHOVIES

¼ cup extra-virgin olive oil

6 garlic cloves, peeled and sliced

12 anchovy fillets

1 cup white wine

3 tablespoons chopped fresh Italian parsley

¼ teaspoon crushed red-pepper flakes

For the polenta: In a large pot, bring 8 cups of water, the olive oil, and salt to a boil. Once the water is simmering, sprinkle in the polenta in handfuls, while whisking to avoid lumps. Take your time sprinkling in the polenta, and whisk well, until all is added and there are no lumps. Bring to a simmer again, and let perk (bubbles will burst forth here and there from the top as the polenta thickens; you want to simmer, not boil). Cook and stir until the polenta is thick and glossy and pulls away from the sides of the pot as you stir, about 30 minutes. Add the chopped scallions. Cover, and keep warm while you make one of the toppings.

For the sardines: Break up the fish into large chunks in a bowl. Add the oil, lemon juice, parsley, and red-pepper flakes, and toss gently. Serve the polenta in a shallow bowl, with the sardine mixture over the top.

For the anchovies: In a medium skillet, over medium-high heat, heat the olive oil. When the oil is hot, add the garlic. Once the garlic is sizzling, add the anchovies. Cook and stir until they dissolve into the oil, about 2 minutes, then add the wine. Bring to a simmer, and cook until reduced by about half, 3 or 4 minutes. Stir in the parsley and red-pepper flakes. Serve the polenta in a shallow bowl, with the anchovy sauce poured on top.

Risotto Wisdom:
Cooking with All Your Senses

I said it all in *Lidia's Family Table,* and I want to repeat it here: risotto requires attention, but once you've got the technique and understanding of making risotto, it is yours to keep for life.

I love making risotto for family meals. It's not something I have time for every day—it takes a good 20 minutes, mostly at the stove—but it is one of those special dishes that focus my attention and engage all my senses in the amazing processes of cooking. I smell, see, and taste what's in the risotto pan, of course, but I am listening, too: for the clicking sound that tells me the rice grains are sufficiently toasted and it's time to splash them with wine; for the distinctive bubbling, as each addition of cooking liquid disappears in the pot, which tells me the rice is ready for more.

If I've stepped away from the stove—I do take a break from stirring risotto now and then, and you can, too—that sound brings me back. I add more liquid and stir, and feel, through the wooden spoon in my fingers, the corner of the pan where the rice is almost sticking, the resistance that tells me yet another cup of broth is needed, before I wander away again.

The Basic Risotto recipe that follows will give you this marvelous engagement of the senses. Its simple formula will let you focus on the critical steps in cooking—in the end, creating a great risotto is 100 percent technique—rather than on a long list of ingredients. You can make this right out of the cupboard, building flavor and superb texture with just olive oil, onions, rice, wine, water, salt, and cheese. Nothing

(continues)

else, not even butter, is necessary. I give you choices, though: use butter or leeks or broth if you want, or use more or less of the ingredients listed in ranges. I want you in the driver's seat, following your senses and tastes, to achieve the texture and flavor you like best.

With risotto, you see, it is more important that you understand what you are doing than that you add things in prescribed amounts. When you are in control of what's happening in the pot, you will feel how powerful a few ingredients and a few techniques can be in creating an outstanding dish.

To sharpen your focus, you'll find each step of the recipe instructions accompanied by a brief explanation of its purpose and the chemistry of risotto—these are short, and, believe me, you will have plenty of time to read them while you are stirring! I love teaching about this precious treasure of Italian cooking.

BASIC RISOTTO
Risotto

Makes about 8 cups risotto, serving 6 or more

5 to 7 cups Chicken Stock (page 55), Simple Vegetable Broth (*Lidia's Italian Table,* page 81), or find stock recipes at www.lidiasitaly .com

4 tablespoons extra-virgin olive oil

2 cups fairly finely chopped onions, leeks, shallots, or scallions (about 10 ounces)

1 teaspoon kosher salt

2 cups short-grain Italian rice, either Arborio or Carnaroli

1 cup white wine

FOR FINISHING

2 tablespoons extra-virgin olive oil or 2 tablespoons butter

½ to 1½ cups freshly grated Parmigiano-Reggiano or Grana Padano

Freshly ground black pepper, to taste

You will need a 3-to-4-quart heavy saucepan, at least 10 inches wide, to allow for steady evaporation. Enameled cast-iron or heavy-gauge stainless-steel pans with a heat-dispersing bottom layer are particularly well suited for risotto.

Pour 7 cups of cooking liquid into a large pot, and bring it almost to a boil. Cover, and keep it hot over very low heat, on a burner close to the risotto pan.

COOKING THE ONIONS

In this stage of cooking, you are softening and caramelizing the onions to form a flavor base for the risotto. You are keeping them from getting brown or crisp, and softening them by cooking in stock, so that they will ultimately melt into the risotto. You then cook off the stock completely, to prepare for the next step, toasting the rice.

Put the oil, onions, and ½ teaspoon of the salt in a big pan, and set over medium heat. Cook the onions slowly, stirring frequently with a wooden spoon, as they sweat, soften, and gradually take on a golden color, 8 to 10 minutes. Adjust the heat if the onions are about to get brown.

Ladle ½ cup of stock into the onions, stir well, and continue to cook the onions without letting them brown, still over low to medium heat, for another 5 to 10 minutes. The onions should be golden and glistening with oil, but all the stock must be cooked away.

TOASTING THE RICE

In this critical step, every grain of rice becomes coated with oil and is slightly toasted in the hot oil. This forms a light covering on the outer layer of each grain that will prevent it from absorbing too much liquid too fast and possibly disintegrat-

(recipe continues)

ing. "Toasting" means that the rice must be cooked on the outside—not browned. Toasted rice will still look white, but you can hear a clicking sound when you stir it.

When the onions are completely devoid of liquid, add the rice all at once, raise the heat to medium, and stir constantly with the oily onions. Cook for about 3 minutes, until the rice grains have been toasted, but do not allow them to scorch or color. Have the wine ready to add.

WHY I USE WINE IN THE RISOTTO

In this quick step, you are balancing the starchy character of the rice with the acidity and taste components of dry white wine. The wine is quickly absorbed by the rice kernels, while the alcohol cooks off. Rice that is not tempered with the addition of wine has less flavor and yields a starchier risotto.

To achieve the best results pour in the wine all at once, and cook with the rice for 2 to 3 minutes, over medium heat. Stir constantly all around the pan, until the wine has been absorbed and the alcohol evaporated. Have the hot stock or water close by, and be ready to add it with a ladle or measuring cup to the rice, and continue making the risotto.

CREATING THE CREAMY RISOTTO

For the next 15 to 20 minutes, the gradual addition of hot stock (it must be hot!) has two effects on the rice: it draws out the starches stored in the kernels, just a bit at a time, while the kernels are slowly absorbing liquid and cooking. Short-grain Italian rice has an abundance of a particular starch that, when released by the kernels into the warm liquid and fat in the pot, forms a creamy suspension. You must maintain a steady, gentle simmering to maintain this process of "amalgamation." While some of the liquid is absorbed by the rice, some is evaporating, and the risotto will thicken and heat up rapidly. You stir continuously to prevent the starches from scorching. And you must add more liquid in small amounts to continue the process as described, until you have reached optimal softening of the kernels and development of the suspension.

It is OK to stop stirring and leave the rice shortly after each addition of liquid, when it is wet and the danger of scorching is minimal—but don't go far.

For the first addition, ladle in 1½ to 2 cups of the very hot liquid, enough to barely cover the rice; stir it in continuously, all around the pan. Add the remaining ½ teaspoon of salt, and stir well. Lower the heat, if necessary, to maintain a very gentle perking.

Stir frequently at first, and then constantly as the risotto thickens. Make sure the spoon is reaching into all the corners of the pan, on the pan bottom, and around the sides. When all the water has been absorbed, the risotto is harder to stir—the bubbling sounds thicker, too—and the pan bottom is visible in the track of the spoon. Ladle in another 2 cups of hot water or stock.

Cook, stirring always, and add another 2 cups of water when the risotto is ready for it, as just described—anywhere from 3 to 6 minutes between additions. Keep track of how much liquid you have added.

FINISHING THE RICE

In this final step, you stop the cooking when the risotto reaches the consistency you want. You finish with olive oil or butter, as a flavoring and amalgamating agent, and incorporate grated cheese and fresh pepper as flavor elements, to taste.

After the addition of at least 5 cups of hot water or stock, you can taste and gauge the degree of doneness of the rice kernels and the fluidity of the creamy suspension. At any time when you find the rice grains pleasantly al dente and the risotto creamy, you can choose to stop cooking. Or you may incorporate more stock, up to about 7 cups total, if you want a softer, looser risotto.

When you are satisfied, turn off the heat and vigorously stir in the 2 tablespoons of olive oil or butter. Stir in grated cheese and freshly ground black pepper to taste. Serve the risotto immediately in heated bowls, with more cheese and pepper at the table.

The Basics of Risotto

The Liquid Used

Some people are surprised to learn that you can make risotto with plain water. Of course you can, since the chemical processes are the same whatever liquid you use. If you have broth of any kind, and you want its particular flavor in your dish, use it. It will impart more flavor, but simple water will do.

The Aromatics

Onions, cooked properly, provide a fine sweet base of flavor for simple risotto, but greater and more complex flavors will come if you add chopped leeks, shallots, and scallions. Shallots have a strong initial flavor but they mellow during cooking and they completely disappear in the risotto. Leek pieces will not disappear, but they add lovely flavor, as do scallions. You can add up to 2 cups of leeks, scallions, or shallots to the pan, after the onions have started to sweat and wilt. But all moisture should be cooked out of them before toasting the rice. For each additional cup of onions, add 1 tablespoon of olive oil.

The Amount of Liquid

There's no set amount—but a general guideline for liquid is three and a half times the amount of rice; the liquid, whether water or stock, should be hot and ready on the stove. The amount of liquid needed may vary because it will evaporate at different rates in different pans and with different heat intensities. What is important is to add liquid until you have produced a risotto with the texture you like.

The Finishing Touches—*Mantecare*

It is important to understand that both olive oil and butter have the amalgamating property—bringing everything together texturally—that is always needed as a "finish" for risotto (this process, to cook until creamy, is referred to as *mantecare* in Italian). Many people mistakenly think that butter—and lots of it—is always required as the finish, to make risotto creamy. (And some chefs whip in butter to give risotto creaminess when it wasn't developed through proper cooking technique.) But our basic recipe shows that you develop the creaminess by the slow release of starch and proper cooking. Olive oil at the end adds a nice complexity that does not alter the essential flavor of the risotto: it is a clean, pristine finish. I like to use olive oil as a finish for fish risotti and some vegetable risotti, because it leaves the clean flavors of the fish and vegetables pure and vibrant.

Butter, on the other hand, is a marvelous liaison: it makes the risotto even creamier and buttery. I use it with all meat or mushroom and some vegetable risotti. The butter makes the dish rich and creamy, magnifying and to some extent altering the flavor. This can be desirable, and there are many risotti in which I love to use it.

LETTUCE RISOTTO

Risotto alla Lattuga

Risotto is always a delicious option for dinner, but for those times when you have nothing to flavor your risotto with, look in the salad bin of your refrigerator and make a great risotto with your salad greens. Lettuce is recommended in this recipe, but another great, economical version is with the tougher outer leaves of any salad green you have in the refrigerator. Use the tender, heart part of the greens to toss a green salad that you can serve alongside the risotto. You will have a balanced and delicious meal, and you will have found a use for everything, wasting nothing. I feel a great sense of accomplishment when I use every morsel of food. I hate waste.

Serves 6

7 cups or more hot Chicken Stock, preferably homemade (page 55)

Kosher salt

¼ cup extra-virgin olive oil

1 cup chopped onion

1 cup chopped leek, white and light-green parts only

2 cups Arborio rice

1 cup white wine

8 ounces outer lettuce leaves (romaine, Bibb, etc.), shredded

2 tablespoons unsalted butter, cut into pieces

½ cup grated Grana Padano or Parmigiano-Reggiano

Bring the chicken stock to a simmer in a medium saucepan, and season with salt.

Heat the olive oil in a large, shallow, straight-sided pot over medium heat. Once the oil is hot, add the onion and leek, sauté for 1 minute, then ladle in ½ cup hot stock to soften the vegetables. Cook until the vegetables are tender and stock has evaporated, about 5 minutes. Raise the heat to medium-high. Add the rice all at once, and stir continuously until the grains are toasted but not colored, about 2 minutes. Add the wine, and cook until the liquid is almost absorbed.

Add the shredded lettuce, and cook until wilted, about 2 to 3 minutes.

Ladle in about 2 cups of the stock, stir, and cook until almost absorbed, about 5 minutes. Ladle in 1 more cup of the stock, and again simmer until the liquid is almost absorbed.

Continue cooking and adding stock in this manner until the rice is cooked al dente but still with texture, about 15 to 20 minutes in all. When the risotto is creamy, turn off the heat. Beat in the butter, stir in the cheese, season with salt if necessary, and serve.

Facing page, top: Lettuce Risotto; bottom: Fava Bean and Leek Risotto (page 166)

FAVA BEAN AND LEEK RISOTTO

Risotto con Fave e Porri

This risotto recipe is delicious when fresh favas are in season, but it can be made with frozen favas. It can also be made with frozen or fresh lima beans or any combination of seasonal vegetables. So have fun making up your own combination; just keep in mind the cooking time of each vegetable. Carrots and squash will take longer than peas and asparagus, so add them to the rice accordingly.

Serves 6

4 leeks, white and light-green parts chopped, tough greens reserved

4 pounds fresh fava beans, shelled, or frozen fava beans (about 4 cups)

¼ cup extra-virgin olive oil

1 cup chopped onion

1½ teaspoons kosher salt

2 cups Arborio rice

1 cup dry white wine

1 tablespoon unsalted butter

½ cup grated Grana Padano or Parmigiano-Reggiano

Put the tough leek greens in a saucepan with water to cover (about 2 quarts), and bring to a simmer while you prepare the other ingredients. Bring a saucepan of salted water to a boil. Add the shelled fava beans, blanch to loosen the skins, about 2 minutes, then cool in an ice bath. Once they're cooled, peel the outer skins from the favas. You should have about 3¼ to 4 cups peeled favas.

Heat the olive oil in a large, shallow, straight-sided pot over medium heat. When the oil is hot, add the onion and chopped leek. Season with 1 teaspoon of salt. Cook until the onion and leek are softened, about 6 minutes.

Raise the heat to medium-high. Add the rice all at once, and stir continuously until the grains are toasted but not colored, about 2 minutes. Add the wine, and cook until the liquid is almost absorbed.

Ladle in about 2 cups of the simmering leek stock, stir, and cook until the liquid is almost absorbed, about 5 minutes. Ladle in 2 more cups of the stock, and add the shelled, blanched favas. Stir and cook in the same manner until the liquid is almost absorbed. Continue cooking and adding water in this manner until rice is al dente, about 15 to 20 minutes in all. You will probably use most, if not all, of the leek stock you made. Season with the remaining salt.

When the risotto is al dente and creamy, turn off the heat. Beat in the butter, stir in the grated cheese, and serve.

CLAM AND SCALLION RISOTTO

Risotto con Vongole e Cipolla Verde

Linguine with clams is an Italian classic and one of my favorite dishes, but this risotto with clams is a wonderful variation, especially with the addition of the scallions. I am from the north of Italy, where risotto is more of the norm than dry pasta, so risotto with seafood is common, especially in the coastal areas. In this recipe, I add the clams in their shells, but you can shuck your clams, reserve their liquid, chop them a bit, then add them and their juice in the last 5 minutes of the risotto-cooking time. Don't add them sooner or the clams will become overcooked and tough.

Serves 6

3 tablespoons extra-virgin olive oil

3 garlic cloves, peeled and crushed

1 cup chopped onion

2 cups Arborio rice

1 cup dry white wine

1 cup crushed San Marzano canned whole plum tomatoes (see page 78)

2 teaspoons kosher salt

2 dozen littleneck clams, scrubbed well

1 bunch scallions, trimmed and chopped (about 1 cup)

3 tablespoons cold unsalted butter, cut into bits

Bring 7 to 8 cups of water or stock to a simmer in a saucepan. Heat the olive oil in a large, shallow, straight-sided pot over medium heat. Once the oil is hot, add the garlic and onion, and cook until the onion is tender, about 5 minutes. Raise the heat to medium-high. Add the rice all at once, and stir continuously until the grains are toasted but not colored, about 2 minutes. Add the wine, and cook until the liquid is almost absorbed.

Add the tomatoes and salt. Bring to a simmer, then ladle in about 2 cups of the water. Stir, and cook until the liquid is almost absorbed, about 5 minutes. Ladle in 1 more cup of water, and again simmer until it is almost absorbed.

Add the clams and another cup of water. Cover, and continue to cook and stir in the same manner until the liquid is almost absorbed. Keep adding water and cooking in this manner until rice is al dente and clams have opened, about 15 to 20 minutes in all. Once the clams start to open, stir in the scallions and turn off the heat. Beat in the butter and serve.

GARLIC RISOTTO
Risotto all'Aglio

Garlic is not often used in flavoring a risotto; onion is usually used as a base flavoring element. In this recipe, however, the flavor of garlic is pronounced, and I love it. It is simple and also delicious, especially if you add some shrimp (or scallops or clams) in the last 5 minutes of cooking. You can also add a vegetable, such as broccoli or peas. Risotto should be served immediately: it continues to cook even after it's taken off the fire, and the rice will become mushy. There is nothing worse for an Italian than overcooked rice or overcooked pasta.

Serves 6

7 cups or more Chicken Stock, preferably homemade (see page 55)

Kosher salt, to taste

14 large garlic cloves, peeled and crushed

1 cup white wine

5 tablespoons extra-virgin olive oil

2 small onions, chopped

2 cups Arborio rice

2 tablespoons unsalted butter, cut into cubes

½ cup grated Grana Padano or Parmigiano-Reggiano

Bring the chicken stock to a simmer in a medium saucepan, and season with salt. In a blender or food processor, purée the garlic and white wine.

Heat the olive oil a large, shallow, straight-sided pot over medium heat. Once the oil is hot, add the onions, and cook until they are tender, about 5 minutes. Raise the heat to medium-high. Add the rice all at once, and stir continuously until the grains are toasted but not colored, about 2 minutes. Add the wine-garlic purée, and cook until the liquid is almost absorbed.

Ladle in about 2 cups of the stock, stir, and cook until the liquid is almost absorbed, about 5 minutes. Ladle in 2 more cups, and again simmer until the liquid is almost absorbed.

Continue cooking and adding stock in this manner until rice is al dente, about 15 to 20 minutes in all. Turn off the heat, beat in the butter, stir in the cheese, and serve.

NEAPOLITAN RICE AND MEAT MOLD

Sartù alla Napoletana

Everyone who is into Italian cooking wants to make the perfect risotto. To make a good risotto is not a small feat. It is all about the technique, and taking the time to stand by and stir it. If you want something a little easier, another option is to make a risottolike dish, such as this one. The cooked and flavored rice is baked in individual molds. It is a great recipe to make when you are having a large dinner party. You can make the rice before, stuff the molds, and then put them in the oven when your guests arrive. Then serve it steaming hot. The aroma will enchant your guests.

Serves 6

¼ cup extra-virgin olive oil

½ cup chopped onion

8 ounces sweet Italian sausage, removed from casing

4 cups sliced mixed mushrooms (cremini, button, shiitake, chanterelles)

8 ounces chicken livers, cleaned, trimmed, and finely chopped

1 cup Arborio rice

½ cup white wine

1 teaspoon kosher salt

1 cup canned whole San Marzano tomatoes, crushed by hand (see page 78)

¾ cup frozen peas, thawed

4 tablespoons butter

Fine dried breadcrumbs, for lining the molds

3 large eggs, beaten

1 cup shredded low-moisture mozzarella

1 cup grated Grana Padano or Parmigiano-Reggiano

You will need 6 to 8 soufflé molds.

Preheat the oven to 400 degrees F.

For the rice: In a saucepan, heat 4 cups of water to a simmer. Heat a large, shallow Dutch oven over medium-high heat. Add the olive oil. When the oil is hot, add the onion and sausage. Brown the sausage all over, and add the mushrooms. Cook until the mushrooms wilt, then add the chicken livers and cook through, about 2 or 3 minutes.

Add the rice to the Dutch oven all at once, and stir continuously until the grains are toasted but not colored, about 2 minutes. Add the wine, and cook until the liquid is almost absorbed. Add the salt and tomatoes, and return to a simmer.

Ladle in about 1 cup of the simmering water, and cook and stir until almost absorbed, about 5 minutes. Ladle in 1 more cup of water, and cook and stir in the same manner until the liquid is almost absorbed. Continue cooking and adding water in this manner until the rice is al dente, about 15 to 20 minutes in all. You will probably use most, if not all, of the water. Stir in the peas, and scrape the mixture onto a sheet pan to cool. While the rice cools, butter the forms and line with breadcrumbs.

Transfer the cooled rice into a large bowl, and stir in 3 beaten eggs, the mozzarella, and the Grana Padano or Parmigiano-Reggiano.

Fill the buttered and breadcrumb-lined soufflé molds. Pack rice in tight. Set on a sheet pan and bake for 40 minutes.

Remove from oven and invert onto serving plate.

FISH

The best wisdom I can give you about fish is that it must be fresh. Here is what to look for when you are buying fish:

If you are buying fresh tuna or swordfish, or, for that matter, any large cut of fish, always look for the blood lines. Make sure they are bright red and not brick color or brown—bright red in the blood lines is an indication of freshness. If you are buying a smaller whole fish, look at the eyes; they should be clear and bulging. If they are cloudy and sunk into the head cavity, the fish is old. Also, take a look at the gills. If they are bright red, like the blood lines, they are fresh. Dark-red or brown gills are an indication that the fish is not fresh. The flesh of a fresh fish is firm to the touch and has a sheen. But your best tool to identify freshness in fish is your nose. If it smells of the sea, buy it. If it smells fishy, then move on.

Once you have bought the fish, there are ways of keeping it fresh.

Fish can go bad very quickly, and that is why it is so important to store it correctly. Temperature is the most important aspect of storing fish. The ideal range for properly storing fish is between 30 and 34 degrees. If you choose to store it in your home refrigerator, which is usually around 41 degrees, you'll cut the shelf life of the fish in half. Fish is best stored on a bed of crushed ice. If that is not an option, you can store the fish on ice cubes. Whenever you store fish on ice, cubed or crushed, keep the fish in a plastic bag, and make sure to keep it out of pools of melted ice water. Freezing the fish immediately is a way of keeping it from spoiling, but when it's defrosted, the texture and juiciness of the fish suffer some.

In this book, I give you a lot of baked and pan-sautéed fish recipes. These techniques are convenient, fast, and tasty. I love grilled fish as well, and here are some general rules for grilling fish:

Grilling is a great method of cooking, especially in the warm spring and summer months. To be sure your grill is clean, scrape the rack well. Marinate your seafood in garlic and oil, and toss in some fresh herbs, such as thyme. Let your fish marinate for about an hour before putting it on the grill. When you are ready to start cooking, make sure you grease the hot grill rack lightly, with an oiled paper towel, before putting on the fish. Grill the fish without turning until it is deeply marked on one side by the grill, from 5 to 10 minutes, or more, depending on fish size. Turn the fish only once; this will minimize sticking. Keep garlic oil handy, and drizzle or brush the olive oil on the fish, but avoid spilling any oil onto the lava rocks or coals, because that will cause flare-ups.

I particularly enjoy eating a whole fish on the bone, with the head and tail attached. The meat around the bones is always sweeter and tastier. I especially like the cheeks and the tail meat. A whole fish, grilled or baked with a drizzle of good extra-virgin olive oil and a squeeze of lemon, is sublime in its simplicity. In preparation for grilling, toss the whole fish with some salt, drizzle it with olive oil, stuff the belly cavity with a few slices of lemon, and set it on the hot grill. Do not touch the fish until it has formed a crust underneath, about 10 to 15 minutes; then flip with a long spatula and cook for an additional 10 minutes on the other side. Or, if you prefer baking the fish, lightly oil a sheet pan, season fish in the same fashion, and bake in a 450-degree oven for 20 to 30 minutes depending on the size. Serve with a sprinkle of coarse sea salt and a drizzle of the best extra-virgin olive oil you have.

RAZOR CLAMS WITH GARLIC AND PARSLEY

Cannolicchi Aglio e Prezzemolo

Razor clams are delicious, but their shells are very fragile, and they overcook easily. The best way to cook them is in a shallow, wide pan, where they can be nestled next to each other all in the same direction; you can stir them gently without breaking the shells. Razor clams might not always be available from your fishmonger, but regular littleneck clams or mussels are a good alternative. Just keep in mind the cooking time of each; mussels cook at about the same speed as the razor clams, whereas the regular clams will take a few more minutes to open.

Serves 4

4 pounds razor clams or mussels or littleneck clams (see headnote)

¼ cup extra-virgin olive oil

8 garlic cloves, peeled and sliced

1 cup white wine

¼ teaspoon crushed red-pepper flakes or 1 whole dried red pepper

2 tablespoons chopped fresh Italian parsley

2 tablespoons fine dried breadcrumbs

If using razor clams, take care, because they can be very sandy. Place the razor clams under cold running water for 15 minutes. Gently wash, taking care not to break the shells, but making sure to get all the sand out. Mussels just need to be washed, scrubbed, and debearded.

In a large Dutch oven, over medium-high heat, heat the olive oil. When the oil is hot, add the garlic. Once the garlic begins to sizzle, pour in the wine. Bring the wine to a rapid simmer, sprinkle in the red-pepper flakes, and add the razor clams or mussels. Cover, and cook until they open, about 6 minutes for razor clams and mussels, and about 8 to 10 minutes for littleneck clams.

Sprinkle with the parsley and breadcrumbs, return to a simmer, stir gently, and serve.

Have plenty of crusty or grilled bread to dunk in the sauce, and if you have any leftovers, pick the clams out of the shells, return them to the sauce, and use it as a dressing for pasta.

SCALLOP SALAD

Insalata di Capesante

This preparation is a delicious main course, especially in the summer, but also makes a delightful appetizer. Scallops are easy to handle. If you want to add an extra touch to the salad, render some bacon slices very crisp, let them cool, and then crumble them on top just before serving. Scallops are indicated in this recipe, but shrimp would be delicious as well.

Serves 6

1½ pounds sea scallops, side muscle or "foot" removed (about 1½ pounds)

7 tablespoons extra-virgin olive oil

1 teaspoon kosher salt

8 ounces Belgian endive (about 2 heads), cut into 1-inch chunks on the bias

8 ounces watercress, leaves and tender stems only (about 1 bunch)

3 hard-boiled eggs, peeled and coarsely chopped

Juice of 1 lemon

Freshly ground black pepper

If your scallops are very thick, halve them crosswise so they will cook quickly. In a bowl, toss the scallops with 3 tablespoons oil and ½ teaspoon salt. Heat a large nonstick skillet over high heat. When the skillet is hot, add the scallops, and sear them on both sides until just cooked through, only a minute or two in all, depending on the thickness of the scallops. Remove the scallops to a plate.

In a large bowl, toss together the endive, watercress, and eggs. Drizzle with the lemon juice and remaining 4 tablespoons of olive oil. Season with the remaining ½ teaspoon of salt and some black pepper. Toss well.

To serve, mound the dressed greens on each plate or a platter, and serve the scallops on top.

QUICK TIP

I would recommend that you buy divers' scallops or dry sea scallops, scallops that are harvested individually rather than dragged. Both are of superior quality and usually not processed, and they'll caramelize better when seared.

SCALLOPS, MUSHROOMS, AND SCALLIONS

Capesante Saltate al Funghi

Serves 6

¼ cup extra-virgin olive oil

6 garlic cloves, peeled and sliced

8 cups sliced mixed mushrooms (button, shiitake, cremini, and chanterelles)

1 teaspoon kosher salt

2 bunches of scallions, trimmed and roughly chopped (about 2 cups)

6 fresh thyme sprigs

2 tablespoons unsalted butter

1¼ pounds sea scallops, foot or side muscle removed

Good-quality balsamic vinegar; Tradizionale Balsamic Vinegar is best for drizzling (optional)

In a large nonstick skillet, over medium-high heat, heat 3 tablespoons of olive oil. Add the garlic, and once the garlic begins to sizzle, add the mushrooms and season with ½ teaspoon salt. Cook until the mushrooms wilt, about 6 to 7 minutes.

Add the scallions, thyme, and butter, and cook until the mushrooms are tender, another 3 or 4 minutes. Transfer to a serving platter, and keep warm.

Wipe out the skillet, return it to medium-high heat, and add the remaining tablespoon of olive oil. Season the scallops with remaining ½ teaspoon of salt, and cook, turning once, until just cooked through, about 1 to 2 minutes per side. Serve on mushrooms, drizzled with balsamic vinegar if desired.

Fish Cooked with Vegetables

In Italy, many fish preparations and sauces include vegetables such as mushrooms and scallions (see Scallops, Mushrooms, and Scallions, page 177, or Halibut Baked with Mushrooms, page 195). Mushrooms bring lots of flavor and moisture to fish. Olives and capers are another classic fish combination (see Codfish with Olives and Zucchini, page 179; Halibut Fillets with Fennel, page 187; or Baked Swordfish, page 192). Tomatoes could be added to any of the above recipes, just as they are paired with grouper (see page 198). Not only does this enhance flavor, but it ends up providing a balanced meal, including protein, starch, and vegetables all in one preparation. Remember, when cooking fish next time: make garlic and extra-virgin olive oil a flavor base, but feel free to add some favorite seasonal vegetables.

CODFISH WITH OLIVES AND ZUCCHINI

Merluzzo alle Olive e Zucchine

This easy way to prepare fresh cod fillets yields a dish full of flavor. Fish, like produce and fruits, is seasonal, and it is best when the fish is running in season—even better if the fish is running locally, in the waters nearest to you. Unlike fruit, fish can be in season multiple times during the year. So, although this recipe is good and traditional prepared this way, you can substitute a local fish like striped bass, flounder, or halibut, that is running and is fresher and cheaper. Just always keep in mind the texture and thickness of the fish fillet, and hence the cooking time.

Serves 6

6 thick pieces skinless cod fillet, about 5 ounces each

¼ cup extra-virgin olive oil

1½ teaspoons kosher salt

2 cups whole cherry tomatoes

8 ounces medium zucchini, sliced into ¼-inch-thick half-moons

½ cup mixed pitted olives, halved

½ loosely packed cup fresh basil leaves, chopped

Preheat the oven to 425 degrees F. Season the cod on a plate with 2 tablespoons of the olive oil and 1 teaspoon of the salt. In a medium bowl, toss the cherry tomatoes, zucchini, olives, and basil with remaining 2 tablespoons of olive oil and ½ teaspoon of salt.

Spread the seasoned vegetables on a rimmed sheet pan. Roast the vegetables on the bottom rack of the oven until they just begin to soften, about 15 minutes. Nestle the seasoned cod in the vegetables, and roast on the middle rack until the fish is cooked through, about 15 to 20 minutes, depending on the thickness of the cod.

Whole live lobsters tend to be intimidating, especially when you need to split them open. In fact, in order for the meat to remain firm, the lobster needs to be alive just before it is cooked. I am sure that most of you have, at some point or other, eaten a mushy, mealy lobster. Most likely that lobster had been dead for a while before being cooked. So, if you wish, set the live lobster in the freezer before splitting it. The lobster is a cold-blooded creature and will become dormant after 30 minutes in the freezer, making it much easier to split. Use clean hand towels or paper towels to hold the lobster while splitting it. Make sure that your cutting board is large enough and set firmly on the counter. Underlay the cutting board with damp paper towels, to hold it in place and absorb the liquid coming from the lobsters.

Use a large chef's knife. Hold a lobster with a towel where the claws meet the body, and twist each claw until it detaches from body. Crack both claws with the back of the knife to make them easier to open when serving. Hold the lobster where the body meets the head, with head facing you. Put the tip of your chef's knife on the lobster's shell about 2 inches or so back from the eyes, and push the knife straight down, through the head, splitting right between the eyes. Turn the lobster around, and proceed to cut the body in half through the tail. Pry the lobster body and tail open into two halves, and clean the body cavity, which is situated behind the eye sockets, the digestive sac, leaving the tomalley (the tasty green digestive part of the lobster). If you see a green sac running along where the body meets the tail, that is the roe and it is delicious. Leave it be. Then proceed to stuff and bake or grill, according to whatever recipe you are using, such as the one that follows.

BAKED LOBSTER WITH
ALMOND-FLAVORED BREADCRUMBS
Aragosta alle Mandorle

Being born on the North Adriatic coast and having an uncle who was a fisherman, as a child I often had fish at home. Lobster, however, not so much. But on those special days when lobster did make it to our table, Grandpa Giovanni would arm us kids with wooden boards and small hammers from his workshop arsenal. We would chew on the small legs and suck all the juice and meat out. But the big front claws were the challenge, especially around the knuckle part. We cracked every single corner of those claws—not a morsel got away. After we were finished, the local cats got their chance. I always wondered if those cute cats ever did find anything in the lobster shells we left behind.

Serves 6

LOBSTERS

Three 1½-pound live lobsters

1½ cups panko breadcrumbs

½ cup blanched, sliced almonds, lightly toasted and coarsely chopped

1 cup grated Grana Padano or Parmigiano-Reggiano

¼ cup chopped fresh Italian parsley

¼ teaspoon kosher salt

¼ cup extra-virgin olive oil

1 cup white wine

SAUCE

6 tablespoons unsalted butter

4 to 6 tablespoons lemon juice

½ teaspoon kosher salt

2 tablespoons chopped fresh parsley

Thirty minutes before you are ready to cook the lobsters, put them in the freezer. Preheat the oven to 400 degrees F. Split the lobsters in half lengthwise, one at a time. Hold each lobster flat on a cutting board, and place the point of a heavy chef's knife through the shell just behind the head, with the blade lined up between the eyes. Bring the blade down firmly, splitting the head in two. Turn the lobster so you can align the knife blade from behind the head along the tail, and cut down through the entire body and tail in one stroke. When all the lobsters are split, remove and discard the sac and nerve tissue in the head cavity, just behind the eyes, and the thin intestinal tract that runs along the back between shell and tail meat. Twist off or cut off the claws with kitchen shears and crack each with the back of a knife or a meat tenderizer to make them easier to open when eating. You will find the green tomalley or possibly green roe which turns orange when cooked (and in English is often called the "coral"). It is all delicious when cooked, so I leave it in, but if you are squeamish you can remove it.

Arrange the six lobster halves and claws on a large, rimmed baking sheet, cut sides up.

In a large bowl, combine the panko, almonds, grated cheese, parsley, and salt. Drizzle with 2 tablespoons of the

(recipe continues)

olive oil, and toss well. Fill the whole length of the lobster cavities with the stuffing, and drizzle the lobsters and claws with the remaining 2 tablespoons olive oil. Pour the wine around the lobster in the baking sheet (but not on the crumbs). Bake, uncovered, until the lobster meat is cooked and the crumbs are crisp, about 20 to 25 minutes.

For the sauce: In a small skillet, melt the butter over medium-low heat. When the butter is melted, whisk in the lemon juice and salt. Sprinkle with the parsley, and stir. Serve the lobsters with the butter sauce on the side.

SALMON FILLETS WITH PROSECCO

Filetti di Salmone al Prosecco

Salmon is a fish not used much in Italy, but the Italians made it their own by cooking it in a light Prosecco sauce.

Serves 4

Four 6-ounce skinless salmon fillets

1¼ teaspoons kosher salt

2 tablespoons extra-virgin olive oil

6 tablespoons unsalted butter

1 bunch scallions, trimmed and chopped (about 1 cup)

1 cup chopped cornichons

2 cups Prosecco

2 tablespoons chopped fresh Italian parsley

Season the salmon with ¼ teaspoon of the salt. Heat a large nonstick skillet over medium-high heat. Add the olive oil. When the oil is hot, add the salmon, and sear it on both sides, about 2 minutes per side, but don't worry about cooking the fish all the way through at this point. Remove the salmon to a plate, pour out the oil, and wipe the skillet clean.

Return the skillet to medium-high heat, and add 4 tablespoons of the butter. When the butter is melted, add the scallions and cornichons, and cook until wilted, about 2 minutes.

Add the Prosecco, and bring to a boil. Boil until reduced by about half, about 5 minutes. Add the remaining teaspoon salt, and slide the salmon back into the sauce. Simmer until salmon is cooked through, about 3 minutes. Whisk the remaining butter and the parsley into the sauce and serve.

SALMON WITH MUSTARD SAUCE

Salmone con Salsa di Senape

Mustard is such a great companion to cooked salmon; it adds a lot of flavor and cuts the fish-oil taste, especially with a little lemon juice and some good dry white wine added to it.

Serves 6

Six 6-ounce skinless salmon fillets

¾ teaspoon kosher salt

2 tablespoons extra-virgin olive oil

6 tablespoons unsalted butter

Juice of 1 lemon

1 cup white wine

2 tablespoons Dijon mustard

¼ cup heavy cream

3 tablespoons chopped fresh Italian parsley

Season the salmon with ¼ teaspoon of the salt. Heat a large nonstick skillet over medium-high heat. Add the olive oil. When the oil is hot, add the salmon, and sear on both sides, about 2 minutes per side, but don't worry about cooking the fish all the way through at this point. Remove the salmon to a plate, pour out the oil, and wipe the skillet clean.

Return the skillet to medium-high heat, and add the butter. When the butter is melted, add the lemon juice and white wine. Bring to a boil, and whisk in the mustard. Lower the flame and let the sauce reduce by a quarter, about 3 minutes; then add the heavy cream and the remaining ½ teaspoon of salt. Slide the salmon back into the sauce. Simmer until the salmon is cooked through, about 3 minutes. Whisk the parsley into the sauce and serve.

HAKE WITH MINT AND LEMON

Nasello alla Mentuccia e Limone

Hake is a light fish. Most soles, fillets of snapper, and bass, all light fish, will also be delicious prepared this way. Keep in mind the size and thickness of the fillets. Each piece should fit on your spatula so you can easily flip it; otherwise, it will fall apart on you. If the fish is thin, wait until the sauce is reduced almost to the finishing point before adding the browned fish, and just bring it to a quick boil.

Serves 6

6 skinless fillets of hake, about
   2½ pounds total

1¼ teaspoons kosher salt

7 tablespoons extra-virgin olive oil

All-purpose flour, for dredging

4 garlic cloves, peeled and crushed

1 medium onion, chopped

1 cup white wine

Juice of 1 lemon

2 tablespoons chopped fresh mint

Heat a large nonstick skillet over medium-high heat. Season fish with 1 teaspoon of salt. When the skillet is hot, add 4 tablespoons of the olive oil, lightly dredge the fish on both sides in the flour, and add the fish to the skillet, skin side down. Brown the hake on both sides, about a minute or two per side, but don't worry about cooking all the way through at this point. Remove the fish to a plate, and wipe out the skillet.

Return the skillet to medium-high heat, and add 2 tablespoons of the olive oil. Add the garlic and onion, and cook until they begin to soften, about 4 minutes. Add the white wine, lemon juice, and remaining ¼ teaspoon of salt. Slide the fish into the sauce, and simmer until it has cooked through, about 4 to 5 minutes more. Stir in the mint, and drizzle with remaining tablespoon of olive oil.

HALIBUT FILLETS WITH FENNEL

Filetti di Ippoglosso e Finocchi

In Italy, fennel is eaten raw, just like celery, dipped in olive oil with salt. It is also cooked in many different ways—used in soups, braised and roasted as a vegetable, or used as a base for a pasta sauce. It has the flavor of licorice and it is credited with assisting in the digestion of a meal.

Serves 6

6 tablespoons extra-virgin olive oil

3 garlic cloves, peeled and crushed

3 medium bulbs fennel, cored, cut into 1-to-2-inch chunks

1 teaspoon kosher salt

½ cup freshly squeezed lemon juice

¾ cup drained tiny capers in brine

2 tablespoons finely chopped fresh Italian parsley

6 skinless halibut fillets, about 2¼ pounds total

In a large skillet, over medium-high heat, heat ¼ cup of the olive oil and add the crushed garlic. Once the garlic is sizzling, add the chunked fennel and season with ½ teaspoon of the salt. Reduce the heat so the fennel caramelizes but doesn't burn. Cover, and cook until the fennel is just beginning to soften, about 5 minutes. Add the lemon juice, cover again, and simmer until the fennel is tender, about 10 minutes. Add the capers, and cook, uncovered, over medium-high heat until the fennel is glazed and caramelized, about 5 minutes more. Stir in the parsley.

While the fennel cooks, season the halibut with the remaining ½ teaspoon of salt. Heat the remaining 2 tablespoons of olive oil in a large nonstick skillet over medium-high heat. Sear the halibut, starting on the side from which the skin has been removed, until the fish is just cooked through, about 2 to 3 minutes per side.

Serve the halibut on a bed of the caramelized fennel.

STRIPED BASS WITH TOMATO PESTO

Spigola con Pesto al Pomodoro

This is a great recipe using the whole fish with heads removed (I often leave them on), but it can be done using bass fillet. If you choose to use fillet, blanch the fennel wedges for 15 minutes, then proceed with the recipe, diminishing the total cooking time of the fish by 15 minutes.

I love fish cooked on the bone, and I love the fish skin when it is crispy, but you can remove it easily once the fish is cooked by picking it off with a fork and spoon before deboning the fish.

Serves 4

1 large bulb fennel, cored, cut into ½-inch wedges

3 teaspoons kosher salt

6 tablespoons extra-virgin olive oil, plus more for the baking sheet

Two 2-pound whole striped bass, cleaned, head removed

5 garlic cloves, peeled and crushed

½ cup white wine

3 ripe plum tomatoes, cored

¼ cup fresh basil leaves

¼ cup fresh Italian parsley leaves

¼ cup whole blanched almonds

Handful fennel fronds

Juice of ½ lemon

Preheat the oven to 400 degrees F. Bring a medium pot of water to a boil, and add the fennel. Blanch until crisp-tender, about 7 minutes, then drain well and season with ½ teaspoon salt.

Oil a rimmed baking sheet with olive oil. Make a bed of fennel on the baking sheet, and put the striped bass on top. Season the fish inside and out with 2 teaspoons of the salt, and put two garlic cloves in the cavity of each fish. Drizzle with the white wine, cover all lightly with foil, and bake for 20 minutes. Uncover, and roast for an additional 20 minutes until the fish is cooked through (skin crispy on the outside, fish tender when pierced with a fork).

Meanwhile, in a food processor, combine the tomatoes, the remaining clove of garlic, the basil, parsley, almonds, fennel fronds, lemon juice, and remaining ½ teaspoon salt. Process to a chunky paste, scrape down the sides of the bowl, and, with the machine running, drizzle in the olive oil to make a slightly chunky pesto. Scrape into a serving bowl, and reserve. When the striped bass is done, remove it with a spatula onto a platter, and debone each fish: open it along the belly part, and gently remove the center bone and all the small bones. Put the fillets of bass and the fennel onto a platter with a spatula, and serve with a dollop of the tomato pesto on top of each piece of fish, and the remaining pesto on the side, so the guests can serve themselves more.

TUNA WITH A MIMOSA SAUCE

Tonno in Salsa Mimosa

Tuna is all about the cooking temperature. I love tuna crudo—*sashimi-quality tuna with a sprinkle of coarse sea salt and a drizzle of extra-virgin olive oil. In this recipe, the tuna is grilled. And if you like your tuna on the raw side, grill it to desired doneness but only on one side; do not flip it on the grill. Serve the nongrilled side up, and top with sauce.*

Then toss a quick salad of arugula, lemon zest, and parsley to dress the grilled tuna, making a delicious and refreshing dish.

Serves 6

Six ½-inch-thick tuna fillets, about
  2¼ pounds total

6 tablespoons extra-virgin olive oil

1½ teaspoons kosher salt

3 loosely packed cups baby arugula,
  coarsely chopped

1 loosely packed cup fresh Italian
  parsley leaves, coarsely chopped

1 lemon, zested in thin strips, juice
  reserved

3 garlic cloves, peeled and crushed

In a large bowl, toss the tuna with 2 tablespoons of the olive oil and 1 teaspoon of the salt. Heat a large cast-iron skillet over high heat. When the skillet is very hot, sear the tuna on one side only, about 3 minutes—you want one side still to remain raw. If you prefer your tuna well cooked, sear 2 minutes on each side. Remove to a cutting board to rest while you make the salad.

In a large bowl, toss together the arugula, parsley, and lemon zest strips. In a small bowl, whisk together the garlic, lemon juice, the remaining ½ teaspoon of salt, and the remaining 4 tablespoons of extra-virgin olive oil. Dress the salad with about half of the dressing, and toss.

To serve, plate the tuna raw side up. Drizzle with the remaining dressing, and top with the salad.

BAKED SWORDFISH

Pesce Spada al Forno

Even though the recipe says this is baked, its taste and texture are more like steamed fish. This is a delightful way to infuse the swordfish with the flavors of the lemon and capers, and a touch of acidity from the vinegar. As with most fish, be careful not to overcook it, since the time varies according to the thickness of the fish.

Serves 6

½ cup dried breadcrumbs

¼ cup grated Grana Padano or Parmigiano-Reggiano

6 tablespoons extra-virgin olive oil

2 tablespoons chopped fresh basil

Six ¾-inch-thick boneless, skinless fillets of swordfish, about 5 ounces each

½ teaspoon kosher salt

6 medium tomatoes, halved at the belly

½ cup white wine

2 tablespoons white-wine vinegar

¼ teaspoon crushed red-pepper flakes

½ cup drained tiny capers in brine

2 tablespoons chopped fresh Italian parsley

Preheat the oven to 400 degrees F. In a small bowl, toss together the breadcrumbs, grated cheese, 2 tablespoons of the olive oil, and the basil. Season the fish with the salt, and rub with 2 tablespoons of the olive oil.

Put the tomatoes, cut side up, on a large, rimmed baking sheet, and drizzle the tomatoes and the baking sheet with the remaining 2 tablespoons of the olive oil. In a measuring cup, combine the wine, vinegar, and red-pepper flakes. Pour around the tomatoes in the sheet pan. Pat about three-quarters of the crumb mixture onto the cut side of the tomatoes. Bake the tomatoes on the middle rack of the oven until they begin to soften, about 10 minutes.

Meanwhile, toss the fish with the remaining crumb mixture. After the tomatoes have baked 10 minutes, scatter the capers and parsley in the pan juices, and fit the swordfish into the spaces in the pan. Bake until the swordfish is cooked through and the crumbs on the fish and tomatoes are browned and crisp, about 15 minutes.

CUTTLEFISH WITH PEAS

Seppie e Piselli

This is one of the most classic ways of preparing cuttlefish. Calamari has made it into American kitchens, but cuttlefish is still a rarity. Cuttlefish is similar to calamari, just a bit wider and meatier. Instead of the cartilage backbone of the calamari, the cuttlefish has a chalky wide internal structure called the cuttlebone. It is the cuttlefish ink sac that is used for black risotto in Italy, not calamari ink. The difference is that when cuttlefish is cleaned and the cuttlebone is removed it opens up, it does not remain a tube like the calamari. It is one of my favorite fish. Have the fishmonger clean it; you'll thank me for that tip. If you insist on doing it yourself, follow the directions below.

Serves 6

6 tablespoons extra-virgin olive oil

1 medium onion, chopped

2 garlic cloves, peeled and crushed

6 ripe plum tomatoes, seeded and diced (strain and reserve juices from seeds; see page 79)

3 cups fresh shelled peas (frozen peas are fine, but add them only 5 minutes before adding the cuttlefish)

¼ teaspoon crushed red-pepper flakes

2 pounds cuttlefish, cleaned and cut

1 teaspoon kosher salt

1 cup white wine

2 tablespoons chopped fresh Italian parsley

In a large skillet, heat 4 tablespoons of the oil over medium heat. Add the onion and garlic, and sauté until fragrant, about 2 to 3 minutes. Add the tomatoes and their juices, the peas, and the crushed red pepper. Cover, and let simmer until the tomatoes release their juices, about 7 minutes.

Push the vegetables to the side of the pan. Pat the cleaned cuttlefish dry, and add head and strips to the skillet. Simmer for a few minutes separately, then mix. Season with the salt, and pour in the wine and remaining 2 tablespoons olive oil. Cover, and let simmer until the cuttlefish are just cooked through (don't overcook), about 7 minutes, mixing occasionally. If desired, pick off any stray skins that have come off the tomatoes. Stir in the parsley, and serve.

QUICK TIP

To clean cuttlefish, pull the head and tentacles, detaching them from the body, and pull out all the innards that come with the head. With a sharp knife, open the back, exposing the wide backbone, and remove the bone. Peel off the remaining skin, and clean any remaining innards. Wash well, and cut into strips like French fries. Cut off any remaining innards attached to the head, and pry out the hard beak in the head. The head is my favorite part. Cut the body in half lengthwise, then cut pieces into ½-inch strips. Cut the head as well in half, leaving the tentacles attached. Wash all well, and let drip-dry.

HALIBUT BAKED WITH MUSHROOMS

Ippoglosso al Forno con Funghi Porcini

I love this dish made with the whole fish, but fillets are much more practical. Halibut is a firm, meaty fish which holds together well when baked with vegetables. On the other hand, you can replace it with your favorite fish fillets (just keep in mind the cooking time will vary with the fish you choose). This dish is best made with porcini mushrooms, but assorted other mushrooms, such as portobello or shiitaki, will also yield good results. If you do not like mushrooms, sliced zucchini is a delicious option.

In cooking fish, especially in the oven, it is important to use the oven heat to your advantage, so you don't overcook the fish but can simultaneously cook the sauce and the vegetables. In this recipe, I tell you to put the fish on the bottom of the oven, because the heat coming from the bottom is greater and will cook the sauce and vegetables faster and not overcook the fish. Also keep in mind that if you want a crispy top you must put the fish or whatever you are cooking on the top shelf of the oven. When you cook on the middle shelf in the oven, the cooking temperature circulates and is distributed evenly around what you are cooking. Shift food around in the oven according to the end results you want to achieve.

Serves 6

4 medium porcini or portobello mushrooms

7 tablespoons extra-virgin olive oil

3 medium onions, thinly sliced

6 garlic cloves, peeled and crushed

1 teaspoon kosher salt

6 skinless halibut fillets, about 2¼ pounds total

Juice of 1 lemon

½ cup white wine

2 tablespoons chopped fresh parsley

Preheat the oven to 400 degrees F. Slice the mushrooms on the bias in 1½-inch-thick slices. Remove the stems from the mushrooms, and shave off the gills if using portobellos. In a large skillet, heat 3 tablespoons of the olive oil over medium heat. Add the onions and garlic, and cook until wilted, about 4 minutes. Spread the onions and garlic on an oiled half sheet pan.

In the same skillet, over medium-high heat, heat 2 tablespoons of the olive oil, and add the mushroom slices (or do in batches if the skillet is too crowded). Drizzle with 2 tablespoons of water. Cook and flip the mushrooms until they are softened and browned, about 4 minutes (per batch, if you're doing it in batches). Spread half of the mushrooms on top of the wilted onions, and season all with ½ teaspoon of salt.

Season the halibut with half of the lemon juice, the remaining ½ teaspoon of salt, and the remaining 2 tablespoons of olive oil. Pour the remaining lemon juice and the white wine over the vegetables, and sprinkle with the parsley. Set the halibut on top, and top each fillet with remaining mushroom slices. Bake the fish on the bottom rack of the oven until it is cooked through and the juices are reduced and saucy, about 18 to 20 minutes.

GROUPER WITH PEPPERS AND POTATOES

Cernia con Peperoni e Patate

Grouper, being a resilient fish of deep waters, does well in this stewlike preparation. In case you cannot find grouper, tilefish or monkfish would be a good alternative. This recipe is a complete meal, with proteins, starch, and vegetables. I like my peppers to be mixed—red, yellow, and green—and I like thicker slices, so they don't overcook. The dish can be made with shrimp and scallops instead of grouper, but if you do make that substitution, add them only in the last 2 to 3 minutes of cooking.

Serves 6

¼ cup extra-virgin olive oil

1 pound Yukon Gold potatoes, peeled, cut into chunks

2 garlic cloves, peeled and crushed

2 red or yellow bell peppers, sliced into ½-inch strips

2 tablespoons tomato paste

¼ teaspoon crushed red-pepper flakes

1½ teaspoons kosher salt

4 fresh thyme sprigs, leaves stripped

1½ pounds skinless grouper, tilefish, or monkfish fillet, cut into 2-inch chunks

2 tablespoons chopped fresh parsley

In a Dutch oven, heat the olive oil over medium-high heat. When the oil is hot, add the potatoes and garlic. Cook and stir until potatoes are golden and crusty, about 10 minutes.

Add the peppers, and cook until they just begin to wilt around the edges, about 3 minutes. Clear a space in the pan and add the tomato paste. Let it toast for a minute or two, then stir the tomato paste into the vegetables. Season with the red-pepper flakes, and add 3 cups water. Bring to a simmer, season with 1 teaspoon of the salt, and add the thyme sprigs. Continue simmering until the potatoes are tender, about 7 to 8 minutes.

Once the potatoes are cooked, season the fish with the remaining ½ teaspoon of salt, and add it to the stew. Gently simmer just until the fish is cooked through, about 5 minutes. Stir in the parsley and serve.

GROUPER WITH TOMATO

Cernia al Pomodoro

Grouper is a deep-water fish, and hence firm in texture; it is delicious baked. Grouper has its seasonality, so cook it when it's running, as the fishermen say. You can replace it in this recipe with other white fish, such as cod, striped bass, or halibut. As always, do keep an eye on the cooking time, which will vary with whatever fish you're using.

Serves 6

6 thick grouper fillets, about 2½ pounds total

3 tablespoons extra-virgin olive oil

1 teaspoon kosher salt

3 garlic cloves, peeled and sliced

1½ pounds medium tomatoes (about 3 to 4 tomatoes), sliced to get 12 slices

¼ loosely packed cup fresh basil leaves, shredded

1 large lemon, thinly sliced to get 12 slices

¼ cup drained tiny capers in brine

¼ teaspoon crushed red-pepper flakes

1 cup dry white wine

Preheat the oven to 400 degrees F. In a bowl, gently toss the grouper with 2 tablespoons of the olive oil and ½ teaspoon of the salt. Use the remaining tablespoon of olive oil to oil the bottom of a large baking dish (10 by 15 inches). Scatter the garlic in the bottom of the baking dish. Make two rows of tomato slices, overlapping, along the long sides of the baking dish. Scatter the basil over the top of the tomatoes, and season all with the remaining ½ teaspoon of salt. Put a piece of grouper on top of two tomato slices, and top each fillet with two thin lemon slices. Scatter the capers in the dish, season with the crushed red pepper, and pour in the wine.

Cover with foil, and bake until the pan juices are bubbling, about 15 minutes. Uncover and move the baking dish to the bottom of the oven, to concentrate the juices, until the fish is cooked through, another 15 minutes or so.

BAKED RICE WITH MUSSELS BARI STYLE

Teglia alla Barese

This is an interesting dish to make because of the combination of two starches. Both absorb the flavors of the mussels and tomatoes, but in different ways. The potatoes absorb the tomato flavor and acidity, while the rice is all about the mussel juice. Mussels are used traditionally in Bari, Puglia. You could use clams or shrimp in this dish, but they do tend to get tough when overcooked, so add the shrimp toward the end of cooking. I also sometimes add chopped zucchini to the rice layer.

Serves 6

1 cup long-grain rice

6 tablespoons extra-virgin olive oil

4 garlic cloves, peeled and sliced

2 pounds mussels, scrubbed and debearded

1 bunch scallions, trimmed and chopped (about 1 cup)

4 large ripe tomatoes, seeded and diced (about 5 cups), with their juices

2 teaspoons kosher salt

2 russet potatoes, peeled, sliced ¼ inch thick

Soak the rice in water to cover for 30 minutes. Preheat the oven to 400 degrees F. In a large (12-inch) tiella- or paella-type pan, heat 2 tablespoons of the olive oil over medium-high heat. Add the garlic. Once the garlic is sizzling, add the mussels, cover, and cook until they just begin to open. Uncover, and let the mussels cook slightly, then remove them from shells. Strain and reserve the cooking juices (about 1 cup).

In a bowl, toss together the scallions, tomatoes, 2 tablespoons of the olive oil, 1 teaspoon of salt, and the mussel meat. Drain the rice, and add it to the bowl. In another bowl, toss together the potatoes, the final 2 tablespoons of olive oil, and remaining teaspoon of salt.

In the same tiella pan, layer half of the potatoes, half of the tomato mixture, the other half of the potatoes, and the remaining tomatoes. Pour over this the mussel-cooking liquid. Cover, and bake 30 minutes, until rice is almost tender. Uncover, and bake until rice is tender and most of the liquid has been absorbed, 20 to 30 minutes more.

MEAT

Understanding Meat

There are many ways of cooking meat: grilling, braising, sautéing, boiling, and roasting are just a few. What is important to understand is the texture and quality of the meat you are cooking. The grading of the meat is also important, especially in red meats; it gives you a sense of what the animal was fed and how long it was aged. Understanding and choosing the right cut of meat for your cooking technique is paramount in meat preparation. You should have periodic discussions with your butcher so you can better understand what you are buying. Today more than ever, when we are so conscious of organic, free-range, natural, grass-fed, hormone-free meats and other products, you should not just buy meat packaged in plastic wrap. The butcher can explain all and talk animal anatomy with you, helping you determine what is the best cut for the recipe you want to prepare. He might even lead you into temptation and have you try some offal, such as liver, sweetbread, or tripe. . . . Yum!!!!

Some basics in cooking meat:

For quick cooking, thin slices are best, usually cooked at high heat and fast. For grilling, a certain thickness, marbling, and fat content are important; it's best to start at a high initial temperature to mark the meat, followed by an even, medium temperature to cook it properly on the inside. For roasting, secondary cuts of meat like shoulders, legs, breasts, ribs, and shanks are the best. All these secondary cuts are less expensive and fall off the bone deliciously when done. In these cuts there is muscle meat with cartilage, which gives you that sticking-to-the-finger goodness. Most of us know that meat around the bone is best. Remember, some fat is needed to keep it all moist and tasty.

So let's talk about roasting. Roasting involves more than sticking a piece of meat in a hot oven. The ingredient list should call for lots of cut-up vegetables, possibly citrus or other fruits, seasonings, and wine and/or broth.

All the vegetables and liquid go into the roasting pan underneath the meat, and all is sealed in a tent of aluminum foil for the first period of cooking in the oven. This I call "wet roasting," and it serves to break down and soften the fibers in the meat and vegetables. As the fibers loosen, they release their flavors. And as the liquid boils and steams within the closed environment, it permeates the meat with all the flavors it has picked up.

The second stage of roasting I call "dry roasting," and it begins when the tent is removed and the meat is exposed to the direct dry heat of the oven. This uncovered cooking produces the crispy and caramelized exterior that we all love and that is an essential part of a roast. It caramelizes the sugars on the meat and the vegetables and reduces the liquids to a viscous, delicious sauce.

Now let's talk about those delicious vegetables and fruits roasting with the meats.

When I roast large cuts of meat, I usually add aromatic vegetables and/or fruits around the meat, to lend flavor to the meat during their hours together in the oven.

I usually mash part of these cooked vegetables and fruit and pass them through a sieve to extract their juices, flavor, and rich pulp to add to the making of the sauce. Most of the time, I put a good amount of vegetables and fruit into the roasting pan with the meat; those that I do not use for making the sauce can be served as the side dish.

Here are some guidelines;

Add dry fruits, such as prunes, apricots, figs, lemons, or oranges, and

(continues)

sturdy root vegetables, such as carrots, parsnips, whole shallots, and ruta-bagas, as well as celery. Cut the vegetables in 3- or 4-inch-long wedges, evenly thick, at least ½ inch wide, or thicker if they must roast a long time. Short wedges cook through, look good, won't break, and caramel-ize on the edges, too.

Cut onions into wedges, but trim them so the layers remain attached at the root end and they don't fall apart.

Cook leeks whole: Use medium-thick leeks (¾ inch) and trim off tough leaves; wash thoroughly; trim the hairlike roots but leave the root base that holds the leaves together. When serving, slice off the root and cut into short lengths.

Use thick celery stalks. Peel to remove tough skin. Cut celery sticks about 1 inch wide.

For oranges and lemons, use the rind without the pith.

After removing the roast and pouring out the pan juices with some of the overcooked vegetables for sauce, return the remaining roasted veg-etables to the roasting pan, and let them get glazed in the hot oven. Then serve them alongside the roast, drizzled with the sauce.

SEARED SESAME CHICKEN BREAST

Petto di Pollo al Sesamo

Sesame seeds are used regularly in Italian baking for desserts and breads, but not as often in the cooking of savory dishes. I find this dish delightful and full of flavor. The chicken is even better if the meat is marinated in the paste for an hour or two, or even overnight.

Serves 6

1 cup oil-packed sun-dried tomatoes, drained

1 cup sesame seeds

2 plum tomatoes, seeded and chopped

1 teaspoon kosher salt

½ cup extra-virgin olive oil, plus more for baking sheet

1 cup grated Grana Padano or Parmigiano-Reggiano

6 boneless, skinless chicken breast halves, sliced on bias into ½-inch-thick medallions

Preheat the oven to 450 degrees F. In a mini–food processor, combine the sun-dried tomatoes, sesame seeds, plum tomatoes, and ½ teaspoon of salt. Process to make a chunky paste. With the machine running, add the olive oil in a slow stream, and process to make a smooth paste. Transfer to a large bowl, and stir in the grated cheese.

Oil a rimmed baking sheet. Season the chicken with remaining ½ teaspoon salt. Toss chicken in bowl with the paste, and pat paste on both sides. Arrange the chicken pieces, not touching, on the baking sheet, patting any extra paste on top. Bake until the chicken is crusty and cooked through, about 15 minutes.

CHICKEN BREAST WITH ORANGE AND GAETA OLIVES

Pollo all'Arancia e Olive

Just about everyone loves chicken breast. It is one of the most Googled terms in recipe searches. I also love this recipe when it's done with drumsticks. If you decide to do that, make sure to double the wine and increase the cooking time until the chicken is done.

Serves 6

2 tablespoons extra-virgin olive oil

1½ pounds thinly sliced chicken cutlets

1 teaspoon kosher salt

All-purpose flour, for dredging

2 tablespoons unsalted butter

1 large red onion, sliced

1 cup pitted Gaeta or Kalamata olives, whole or halved

Juice and grated zest of 1 orange

½ cup white wine

1 teaspoon fennel powder

2 tablespoons chopped fresh Italian parsley

In a large skillet, over medium heat, heat the olive oil. Season the chicken with ½ teaspoon of salt, and lightly dredge it in flour. Lightly brown the chicken in the skillet (you want the chicken to end up with a blond-colored crust) on both sides, about 2 minutes per side. Cook the chicken in batches if necessary, depending on the size of your skillet. Remove pieces to a plate as they color.

Once the chicken is colored, add the butter and onion and cook until softened, about 3 to 4 minutes. Add the olives, orange juice and zest, white wine, and fennel powder. Put chicken back in the skillet, and simmer until the chicken is just cooked through and the sauce coats the chicken, about 3 to 4 minutes. Season with remaining salt, sprinkle with the parsley, and serve.

> **QUICK TIP**
> To make fennel powder put ½ cup fennel seed in a spice grinder, and mill until you have a fine powder (yields about ¼ cup). Store at room temperature, sealed.

SKILLET GRATIN OF
MUSHROOMS AND CHICKEN

Gratinata di Pollo e Funghi

When you're talking about chicken, everybody today assumes you are talking about chicken breasts. But I happen to feel that chicken breasts can be awfully dry if not cooked properly. This recipe, when done right, retains moisture in the breast, and the combination of ingredients gives it a rich and savory complexity of flavors. All you need to serve with it is a tossed salad, and you have a complete meal.

Serves 6

6 medium boneless, skinless chicken breasts (about 6 ounces each)

1 teaspoon kosher salt

All-purpose flour, for dredging

4 tablespoons unsalted butter

4 tablespoons extra-virgin olive oil

12 large shiitake mushrooms, stems removed

3 garlic cloves, peeled and crushed

6 fresh sage leaves

½ cup white wine

½ cup prepared tomato sauce

6 tablespoons grated Grana Padano or Parmigiano-Reggiano

Pound the chicken to about ½-inch thickness (or butterfly to the same thickness). Season the chicken with ½ teaspoon of salt. Dredge the chicken lightly in the flour and tap off any excess. In a large cast-iron skillet, melt 2 tablespoons butter in 2 tablespoons of the olive oil over medium heat. Lightly brown the chicken on both sides, about 2 minutes per side, then remove to a plate.

Once the chicken is out of the skillet, add the remaining 2 tablespoons of olive oil, mushroom caps, and garlic. Season with the remaining ½ teaspoon of salt. Drizzle with ¼ cup of water, and cook until the mushrooms are softened and the water evaporates, about 4 minutes.

Slide the mushrooms to the side, and put the chicken back in the pan, in one layer, and arrange two mushroom caps on top of each piece. Increase the heat to medium-high, and add the sage leaves and the remaining 2 tablespoons of butter, in pieces, in the spaces in the pan. Pour the white wine and tomato sauce into the spaces in the pan as well. Sprinkle each chicken breast with 1 tablespoon of the grated cheese. Cover, and simmer until the chicken is cooked through, about 10 minutes. Uncover, increase heat to reduce the sauce to your liking, and serve.

CHICKEN WITH CAPERS AND ANCHOVIES

Pollo e Capperi e Acciughe

Capers and anchovies are a great blend of flavors. They are delicious when used to dress pasta, braise a pork chop, or sauté with fish. In this recipe, they bring a lot of complexity and flavor to the chicken. You could substitute chicken wings or drumsticks for a whole chicken.

Serves 6

One 5-pound roasting chicken, skin on

2 teaspoons kosher salt

3 tablespoons extra-virgin olive oil

8 anchovies, chopped

6 garlic cloves, peeled and sliced

Juice of 2 lemons (about 6 tablespoons)

½ cup white wine

½ cup drained tiny capers in brine

1 tablespoon chopped fresh Italian parsley

Cut the chicken into sixteen pieces as follows: two wings, two drumsticks, two thighs, each breast half into three pieces, back and neck into four pieces. Pat the chicken dry, and season with the salt.

In a large cast-iron skillet, heat the olive oil over medium heat. Add the breast pieces, and brown on all sides, a minute or two per side; remove to a plate. Add all of the dark meat, and brown well on all sides, about 10 minutes in all. Drain off and discard all but 1 tablespoon of the fat in the pan.

Add the chicken pieces back to the skillet. Over medium-high heat, add the anchovies and garlic, stirring to dissolve the anchovies in the oil. Pour in the lemon juice and white wine. Bring to a simmer, cover, and simmer for 5 minutes. Uncover, and scatter in the capers. Re-cover, and simmer until the chicken is just about cooked through, about 10 minutes more. Uncover, bring to a rapid simmer, and cook until sauce is reduced and chicken is juicy and tender, about 5 to 10 minutes more. Stir in the parsley and serve.

SPICY BUTTERFLIED CORNISH HENS

Pollo Giovane alla Diavolo

I do not see too many Cornish hens in the poultry department these days. I guess people prefer the large chicken breasts without bones. I feel the meat around the bones is the tastiest, and the Cornish hen certainly has enough bones to pick from. The beauty of this dish is that every portion ends up being a whole Cornish hen, so it's easy and makes for a beautiful presentation. Season, butterfly, and sear; then finish in the oven.

Serves 6

6 Cornish hens, about 1½ pounds each

2 teaspoons kosher salt

½ cup extra-virgin olive oil

6 pickled hot cherry peppers, halved, seeded (if desired), plus ¼ cup brine

8 garlic cloves, peeled and sliced

6 fresh bay leaves

4 fresh rosemary sprigs, needles removed

1 cup white wine

Preheat the oven to 400 degrees F. Remove the wingtips from the hen. With scissors cut out the backbones from Cornish hens (save for stock). Open the hens and press at the breast to flatten them. In a large roasting pan, toss the hens with the salt, olive oil, cherry peppers and brine, garlic, bay leaves, and rosemary. Marinate for 1 hour.

Heat a large cast-iron skillet over medium-high heat. Pour the marinade into a bowl, and mix with the white wine. Sear the hens in the hot skillet in batches to brown on both sides, about 2 minutes per side. As the hens are browned, return them to the roasting pan, and arrange them breast side up, fitting them flat in the pan. Pour the wine with marinade over the hens, and roast on the middle rack of the oven for 30 minutes. Move the pan to the bottom of the oven, and roast until hens are cooked through, the skin is crispy, and the marinade has reduced to a sauce, about 15 minutes more. If the hens are done and the sauce is still too thin, move the hens to a serving platter and reduce the sauce in the pan directly on the stovetop.

LEMON GUINEA HEN

Faraona al Limone

This dish can be made with regular chicken and it will be delicious, but guinea hen has a different, light, gamy kind of flavor. A guinea hen is a noisy chicken that is gray in plumage, dotted with white spots. In Italy it is a special treat because of its extra flavor and is used in holiday cooking. It has the texture of a free-range chicken.

Serves 4

Two 3-pound guinea hens if possible, or chickens

2 teaspoons kosher salt

All-purpose flour, for dredging

7 tablespoons extra-virgin olive oil

8 garlic cloves, peeled and sliced

2 lemons, thinly sliced

¼ teaspoon crushed red-pepper flakes

1 cup white wine

Preheat the oven to 400 degrees F. Cut each guinea hen into four pieces, separating the breasts and leg-thigh portions. Season with salt. Lightly dredge each piece in flour. Heat a large skillet over medium-high heat. Add 3 tablespoons of the olive oil. When the oil is hot, add the hen pieces in batches, and brown on both sides, about 5 minutes per side. Remove the meat to a roasting pan and arrange in one layer.

Pour off the oil from the skillet and add the remaining 4 tablespoons of olive oil over medium-high heat. Add the garlic. Once the garlic is sizzling, add the sliced lemon, and brown the slices on both sides. Add the crushed red-pepper flakes. Pour in the wine and 1 cup of water. Bring to a boil, then pour over the hens in the roasting pan.

Roast the meat, uncovered, for 30 minutes on the middle rack of the oven. Flip each piece and roast for another 30 minutes. Flip once more, and move the pan to the bottom of the oven to reduce and concentrate the sauce; roast for about 10 minutes more. If the sauce is still too thin, remove the meat and reduce the sauce directly on the stovetop for a minute. Serve the hens with sauce.

PAPPARDELLE WITH TURKEY ROLLS

Pappardelle con Involtini di Tacchino

On Sundays, my grandmother Rosa would often make guazzetto *with one of the courtyard hens. She would braise it for hours with onions, tomatoes, and herbs, and then dress pasta with it for dinner. This recipe reminds me of Nonna Rosa's* guazzetto, *although it is a quicker version and made with turkey. You can store the sauce for a few days in the refrigerator or for a week or two in the freezer. Fresh pappardelle is best in this recipe but dried pasta such as fettuccine or spaghetti is delicious as well.*

Serves 6

1 teaspoon kosher salt, plus more for the pot

12 turkey breast cutlets (about 2 pounds total), pounded to an even ½-inch thickness

12 thin slices prosciutto

1 cup grated Grana Padano or Parmigiano-Reggiano

4 tablespoons chopped fresh Italian parsley

5 tablespoons extra-virgin olive oil

All-purpose flour, for dredging

½ cup chopped onion

3 garlic cloves, peeled and sliced

1 cup white wine

One 28-ounce can whole San Marzano tomatoes, crushed by hand (see page 78)

Pinch crushed red-pepper flakes

1 pound fresh (page 145) or dry pappardelle

Bring a large pot of salted water to boil for pasta. Lay the turkey cutlets out on a cutting board, and season with ½ teaspoon of salt. Fit a slice of prosciutto on each cutlet, folding it in if the prosciutto slice is larger than the turkey cutlet. Sprinkle each cutlet with ½ tablespoon of grated cheese and 1 teaspoon of chopped parsley. Roll the cutlets up, starting on the short side, and secure closed with toothpicks.

Heat a large Dutch oven over medium-high heat. Add 3 tablespoons of the olive oil. Dredge the rolls in flour, and tap off the excess. When the oil is hot, add the rolls, and brown lightly on all sides, about 3 to 4 minutes in all. Remove to a plate.

Add the onion and garlic, and cook until the onion is softened, about 5 minutes. Increase the heat, add the wine, and boil until the liquid is reduced by half, about 2 minutes. Add the tomatoes, slosh out the can with 1 cup of water, and add that as well. Adjust the heat so the sauce is simmering, and season with remaining ½ teaspoon of salt and the crushed red pepper. Slide the turkey rolls back into the sauce, and simmer until the rolls are tender and the sauce is flavorful, about 25 minutes.

When the rolls are almost done, start cooking the pasta. Remove the rolls to a plate, but keep them warm. When the pasta is al dente, transfer it with tongs directly to the simmering sauce, and drizzle with the remaining 2 tablespoons olive oil. Toss to coat the pasta with the sauce. Turn off the heat, sprinkle with the remaining grated cheese. Serve the pasta on a platter, surrounded by the turkey rolls, taking care to remove the toothpicks before serving.

VEGETABLE AND MEAT CASSEROLE

Sformato di Verdure e Carne

This is a flavorful, easy, and economical dish that you will cook over and over and your family will love. Here I use turkey, but ground chicken, beef, pork, or veal would work just as well; be sure to adjust the cooking time if you make the switch. If you do not have the time to bake it, just cook this recipe a little longer on top of the stove and it will become a delicious dressing for pasta. This is a satisfying dish to serve for a gathering. It's a one-pot balanced meal, with meat and vegetables; just flank with some potatoes, rice, or polenta.

Serves 6

6 tablespoons extra-virgin olive oil

2 small onions, thinly sliced

1 pound zucchini, diced

2 teaspoons kosher salt

1½ pounds ground turkey

2 tablespoons tomato paste

1½ cups white wine

2 fresh bay leaves

1¾ pounds russet potatoes, peeled and thinly sliced (¼ inch thick or less)

8 ounces low-moisture mozzarella, shredded

1 cup grated Grana Padano or Parmigiano-Reggiano

2 tablespoons unsalted butter, at room temperature

Preheat the oven to 400 degrees F. In a large skillet, heat 3 tablespoons of the olive oil over medium-high heat. Add the onions, and cook until slightly softened, about 3 minutes. Add the zucchini and 1 teaspoon of salt. Cook until the zucchini is tender, then remove vegetables to a plate with a slotted spoon. Add 1 tablespoon of the olive oil to the skillet. When the oil is hot, add the ground turkey. Cook and stir the turkey until it is crumbled and browned, about 4 minutes. Then clear a space in the pan and add the tomato paste. Let it toast for a minute, then stir it into the turkey. Add the wine and bay leaves, bring to a simmer, and cook until the wine is reduced and saucy, about 5 minutes. Stir in the onions and zucchini.

Toss the potato slices with the remaining 2 tablespoons of olive oil and the remaining teaspoon of salt. In a medium bowl, toss together the two cheeses. To assemble, butter a large oval baking dish (4-quart size). Layer the potatoes in the bottom, and sprinkle with a third of the cheese. Layer all of the turkey mixture, then all of the remaining grated cheese. Cover with foil (making sure it doesn't touch the cheese), and bake on the bottom rack until bubbly around the edges, about 20 minutes. Uncover, and bake until the top is browned and crusty, about 15 minutes more.

MARINATED MEATBALLS

Polpettine Marinate

Everybody seems to love meatballs. Here is a different and tasty alternative to their normal red-sauce preparation. These veal or turkey meatballs are marinated in a tangy marinade of herbs and vinegar. They are good for buffet tables, picnics, or just to keep in the refrigerator for a snack. They make terrific sandwiches as well, and if you serve them with some mashed potatoes it becomes a meal.

Makes about 36

MARINADE

3 cups white wine

2 cups balsamic vinegar

2 cups sliced white onion

6 garlic cloves, peeled and crushed

6 fresh sage leaves

2 fresh rosemary sprigs, needles stripped

2 fresh bay leaves

4 whole cloves

½ teaspoon kosher salt

MEATBALLS

1½ pounds ground veal (or turkey)

One 8-ounce piece deli ham, finely chopped

3 large eggs, beaten

1 cup panko breadcrumbs

½ cup grated Grana Padano or Parmigiano-Reggiano

¼ cup chopped fresh parsley

½ teaspoon kosher salt

¼ teaspoon ground cinnamon

Freshly ground black pepper

Vegetable oil, for frying

All-purpose flour, for dredging

For the marinade: Combine all of the ingredients in a medium saucepan. Bring to a boil, and cook at a rapid simmer until reduced to 1½ cups, about 20 minutes.

Meanwhile, for the meatballs: Combine all the ingredients except the flour and vegetable oil in a large bowl, and mix well. Roll the mixture into about three dozen bite-sized meatballs. Flatten slightly into patties. In a large nonstick skillet, over medium-high heat, heat about ½ inch vegetable oil. Lightly dredge the meatballs in the flour, and brown in batches until cooked through, about 8 minutes per batch. Drain the meatballs on a paper-towel-lined plate, and place them in one layer or two snug layers in a serving dish. Strain the marinade over the meatballs. Let them marinate for at least 30 minutes, turning once or twice, before serving. This dish can also be made a day ahead and left to marinate in the refrigerator overnight. Bring to room temperature or reheat before serving.

VEAL WITH ONION AND SQUASH

Spezzatino con Cipolline e Zucca

This is another one-pot complete meal, in which the protein and vegetables come together. In this recipe, veal is recommended, but pork, beef, or lamb could be substituted. As always, just keep the cooking time in mind for the different meats. This is also an economical meal: secondary cuts of meat give the most flavorful results and are cheaper. Here butternut squash and onions are the vegetables but you certainly can substitute according to season and preference. Peppers, carrots, parsnips, and squash could be added but again, as with substituting the meat, keep in mind the cooking time for each different vegetable so you do not get a mushy result.

Serves 6

¼ cup dry porcini mushrooms

2½ pounds veal for stew, cut into 1-to-2-inch cubes

2 teaspoons kosher salt

All-purpose flour, for dredging

¼ cup extra-virgin olive oil

3 tablespoons tomato paste

2 cups pearl onions, peeled

8 sage leaves, chopped

1 cup white wine

1 butternut squash (about 2 pounds), peeled and cut into 1-to-2-inch chunks

Soak the porcini mushrooms in 1 cup of hot water for 30 minutes. Season the veal with 1 teaspoon of the salt. Dredge the veal in flour, and tap off the excess. Heat the olive oil in a Dutch oven over medium-high heat. When the oil is hot, brown the veal on all sides in batches, stirring to let a crust form.

Return all of the veal to the pot, clear a space at the bottom, and add the tomato paste. Let the tomato paste toast for a minute, then stir it into the veal. Add the pearl onions and sage, and brown for a few minutes. Drain the porcini, reserving the soaking liquid; finely chop, and add them to the pot. Pour in the wine, and bring to a simmer. Strain the porcini liquid, and add it to the pot with 1 cup of hot water. Simmer, covered, for 10 minutes; then uncover, add 1 cup of hot water, and cover again. Simmer until the veal is beginning to become tender, about 30 to 45 minutes.

Uncover, and add the squash and ½ cup of hot water. Simmer, covered, until the squash and veal are both tender, about 20 minutes more. Season with the remaining teaspoon of salt, and raise the heat; simmer rapidly to reduce the sauce, if necessary, till it glazes the veal and squash.

CITRUS ROASTED VEAL

Vitello Arrosto agli Agrumi

Whenever you want to bring lightness to your cooking, lemon will do the trick. Whether in desserts, in stuffing, in braising, or, as in this recipe, in roasting, lemon zest and juice bring freshness to any preparation. Veal can be expensive, but using a secondary cut like the shoulder reduces the cost, and, in my opinion, it yields better flavor.

Serves 6 to 8

One 4-to-5-pound bone-in veal shoulder roast

1½ teaspoons kosher salt

3 tablespoons extra-virgin olive oil

2 tablespoons unsalted butter

3 medium onions, peeled and quartered but left attached at the root

1 pound carrots, peeled and cut into 2-inch lengths

1 fresh rosemary sprig, needles stripped

½ cup white wine

Zest and juice of 1 orange

Zest and juice of 1 lemon

1 cup Chicken Stock, preferably homemade (page 55)

Preheat the oven to 400 degrees F. Season the veal all over with 1 teaspoon of the salt. Heat a large, low Dutch oven over medium heat, and add the oil. When the oil is hot, brown the veal on all sides, about 10 minutes in all.

Add the butter. Once the butter melts, drop the onions, carrots, and rosemary around the veal. Season the vegetables with the remaining ½ teaspoon of salt. Pour in the wine and citrus juices, and add the zest. Reduce the liquid by half, then add the stock. Return to a simmer, cover, and roast in the oven until the veal is very tender, about 1½ hours.

Remove the meat to a cutting board, and let rest. Remove the vegetables to a platter. Bring the sauce to a boil, and reduce until thick, if necessary. Thinly slice the veal against the grain, and serve on the platter with the vegetables and sauce.

LONDON BROIL STEAK WITH SUN-DRIED TOMATOES MARINADE

Bistecca con Pomodori Secchi

This inexpensive cut of steak, when marinated and grilled, becomes tender and delicious. The marinade is complex and leaves the steak packed with flavor. If the whole family is coming over, just double the recipe and marinate it overnight, and a tasty and economical meal will be ready for all.

Serves 6

1 cup red wine

½ cup oil-packed sun-dried tomatoes, drained

¼ packed cup fresh basil leaves

4 garlic cloves, peeled and crushed

1 teaspoon kosher salt

¼ teaspoon crushed red-pepper flakes

½ cup plus 2 tablespoons extra-virgin olive oil

One 1¾-pound boneless beef shoulder London-broil steak, about 1 to 1½ inches thick

In a food processor, combine the wine, sun-dried tomatoes, basil, garlic, salt, and red-pepper flakes. Pulse to make a chunky paste. Scrape down the sides of the bowl, and then, with the machine running, pour in ½ cup of the olive oil in a steady stream to make a smooth sauce.

Put the steak in a resealable plastic bag, and pour in the marinade. Marinate in the refrigerator for at least 1 hour or up to overnight.

Preheat the oven to 425 degrees F. Remove the steak from the marinade (but don't pat it dry—let the marinade coat it), and put it in a roasting pan. Drizzle with the remaining 2 tablespoons olive oil, and roast until medium-rare, about 20 minutes. Remove to a cutting board, let rest for 5 to 10 minutes, then thinly slice against the grain and serve.

STUFFED HAMBURGERS

Hamburger Imbottiti

Even the Italians love hamburgers. But in the Italian culture it cannot be only about meat. The Italian meal needs to have balance, so the addition of a little veggie and a little cheese rounds out this meaty meal.

Serves 6

1½ pounds ground beef

½ cup oil-packed sun-dried tomatoes, drained, finely chopped

2 tablespoons balsamic vinegar

1 teaspoon kosher salt

4 ounces low-moisture mozzarella, cut into small cubes

6 large basil leaves, chopped

1 tablespoon extra-virgin olive oil

Ketchup or Hamburger Sauce (page 84), for serving

In a large bowl, combine the ground beef, sun-dried tomatoes, vinegar, and salt. Mix the ingredients together with your hands to combine. Form into six equal-sized balls.

In a small bowl, toss together the mozzarella and basil. Make an indentation in each ball, and press in some of the mozzarella-basil mixture. Seal the mozzarella in, and press to form patties about an inch thick.

Heat a large cast-iron skillet over medium-high heat. Add the olive oil. When the oil is hot, add the patties, and cook until they're cooked through and the cheese inside is melted, about 8 to 10 minutes in all. To check if the cheese has melted inside, stick a toothpick into the center; if the cheese has melted, it will stick to the toothpick. Serve with the homemade ketchup (on a bun or with a salad).

Facing page: Stuffed Hamburger with Hamburger Sauce (page 84)

FILET MIGNON ITALIAN STYLE WITH BALSAMIC REDUCTION

Filetto al Balsamico

Filetto, or filet mignon, is one of the most voluptuous of all beef cuts, and because of its popularity and ease of preparation, there are a great many recipes for it. Here is a zesty Italian way of preparing filet mignon, simple but mouth-watering. In this recipe, the complexity of flavors in the sauce comes from the reduction of the balsamic vinegar.

The traditional balsamic vinegar is delicious but expensive, so when making this reduction, use one of the different offerings of balsamic vinegar you find in the grocery store; it will yield a great sauce. If you feel extravagant and have one of those little precious bottles of the Balsamico Tradizionale—seven years old, aged in wooden casks in the solero method—instead of making the reduction from the commercial balsamic vinegar, just drizzle some of the Tradizionale over the filet.

The Balsamico Tradizionale, made by selected producers, is always sold in the signature bottle with an onionlike base. The bottlers are different, the bottle shape the same and the product sublime.

Serves 8

3 cups commercial balsamic vinegar (see headnote)

2 carrots, peeled and cut into chunks

2 celery stalks, cut into chunks

1 onion, peeled and quartered

2 fresh bay leaves

2 fresh rosemary sprigs, needles stripped

2½-pound piece beef tenderloin, tied

1 teaspoon kosher salt, plus more for serving

1 tablespoon extra-virgin olive oil, plus more for serving

Preheat the oven to 450 degrees F. In the meantime start the balsamic vinegar reduction. In a medium saucepan, combine the vinegar, carrots, celery, onion, bay leaves, and rosemary needles. Bring to a boil, and simmer until the vinegar has reduced by half, about 30 minutes. Strain the vinegar into a clean saucepan, and keep warm. Discard the vegetables and herbs.

Season the beef with salt, and coat with the olive oil. Heat a cast-iron skillet over high heat. When the skillet is hot, sear the beef on all sides, then set the skillet in the preheated oven to roast until medium-rare, about 15 minutes. Let rest on a cutting board for 10 minutes, then slice.

To serve: Once the filet is sliced, sprinkle with coarse salt and drizzle with olive oil, then with a spoon lightly drizzle the filet slices with the balsamic-vinegar reduction.

LAMB STEW WITH SAFFRON AND TOMATOES

Agnello allo Zafferano e Pomodori

Saffron is an expensive seasoning, but a little will go a long way. It is the pistil of the crocus flower, and each strand is hand-plucked from the flower, then dried. I like using the strands, but saffron powder is available as well. To extract the flavor, the saffron is soaked in hot water, then added to the cooking food. It is usually added in the last 20 minutes of the cooking time. In this recipe, I use boneless chunks of lamb shoulder, an economical cut, but I splurge on the saffron. The dish is delicious with the saffron, but if you want to make it without saffron, it's still awfully good.

Serves 6

1 heaping teaspoon saffron strands, or ½ teaspoon saffron powder

¼ cup extra-virgin olive oil

2 pounds boneless chunks lamb shoulder

2½ teaspoons kosher salt

6 garlic cloves, peeled and crushed

¼ teaspoon crushed red-pepper flakes

One 28-ounce can whole San Marzano tomatoes, crushed by hand (see page 78)

Steep the saffron strands in ½ cup of hot water for 20 minutes. Heat the olive oil in a large Dutch oven over medium heat. Season the lamb all over with 1½ teaspoons of salt. When the oil is hot, add the lamb chunks and garlic (don't crowd the pan; do this in batches if necessary), and sear until the meat is browned all over, about 10 minutes.

Season with the red-pepper flakes. Add the crushed tomatoes and remaining teaspoon salt. Slosh the tomato can out with 1 cup of hot water, and add that as well. Bring to a brisk simmer, and simmer, covered, until the lamb is tender, about 45 minutes. Add the saffron and water, and cook uncovered for the last 25 to 30 minutes to reduce the sauce so it glazes the meat. This dish is delicious with some crusty bread, but try it with Mashed Potatoes and Fava Beans (page 90) or with polenta (page 154).

SEARED LOIN LAMB CHOPS WITH RED WINE SAUCE

Scottadito d'Agnello al Vino Rosso

Lamb chops are usually readily available in grocery stores and at the butcher shop. Grilling them is easy, and a good way to keep their flavor. I also like to sear them in a heavy skillet, pressing them down with a spatula so all the surfaces get crisp. Here I recommend loin lamb chops, which are more economical than the rack lamb chops, and just as tasty. Chops are best served rare or medium-rare. I like to make a little wine sauce to serve on the side. This sauce can be made in advance and keeps well in the refrigerator or freezer. It can be frozen in small portions, and reheated when you grill lamb or any other kind of meat. This sauce is great on grilled chicken, or grilled or seared steak or venison.

Serves 6

2 cups dry red wine

½ cup dried cherries

4 garlic cloves, peeled and crushed

3 fresh bay leaves

1 large fresh rosemary sprig

2 teaspoons kosher salt

Freshly ground black pepper

2 tablespoons unsalted butter

12 loin lamb chops, about ¾ inch thick (about 2¼ pounds total)

1 tablespoon extra-virgin olive oil

In a medium saucepan, combine the wine, cherries, garlic, bay leaves, rosemary, and 1 teaspoon of salt. Season with freshly ground black pepper. Bring to a boil over medium-high heat, and boil until the liquid has reduced to about 1 cup, about 10 minutes. Pick out the rosemary, bay leaves, and garlic, and discard. Whisk in the butter. Set aside and keep sauce warm while you cook the lamb.

While sauce reduces, heat a large heavy skillet over medium-high heat. Season the lamb chops on both sides with the remaining teaspoon of salt. Heat the olive oil in the skillet, and when the oil is hot, add the chops and sear to medium-rare, about 2 to 3 minutes per side. Serve with sauce poured over the chops.

APPLE CIDER VINEGAR BRAISED PORK SHOULDER

Spalla di Maiale Brasata al Succo di Mela

Slow-cooking recipes don't require that much attention, and they turn out complex and delicious. The less expensive cuts of meat are usually best for braising. Long-cooked meat is also easier on the digestive system. This is a perfect recipe for a large group, and can be increased without problems. Any leftovers can be turned into pulled pork for sandwiches the next day.

Serves 8

One 4-pound piece bone-in pork shoulder

2 teaspoons kosher salt

⅓ cup extra-virgin olive oil

2 pounds small (not baby) turnips, peeled and quartered

6 garlic cloves, peeled and crushed

½ cup apple cider vinegar

2 cups white wine

2 cups apple cider

2 fresh rosemary sprigs, needles stripped

6 fresh sage leaves

Season the pork shoulder all over with 1 teaspoon of the salt. Heat a large Dutch oven over medium-high heat. Add the olive oil. When the oil is hot, add the turnips, and sear them on all sides, about 4 to 5 minutes. Remove to a plate. Add the pork and garlic, and brown the pork well on all sides, about 8 to 10 minutes.

Add the vinegar, bring to a boil, and reduce the liquid by about half. Add the white wine, cider, rosemary, sage, and 2 cups of water. Bring to a simmer, and season with remaining teaspoon of salt. Cover, and simmer until the pork is beginning to become tender, about 1 hour and 45 minutes.

Uncover, add turnips, and cover again. Cook until the turnips and the pork are very tender, about 45 minutes more, uncovering for the last 5 to 10 minutes to reduce the sauce to a glaze. The pork shoulder can be sliced or shredded. Serve with the turnips and pan juices.

PORK AND PRUNE KABOBS

Spiedini di Maiale alle Prugne

The savory-and-sweet combination of fruit and meat together satisfies me; the fruit renders the meat lighter. Here I use prunes—Italians love prunes. Of course, you can substitute your favorite dried fruit, or fresh fruit in season. In the recipe, I suggest cooking them in a cast-iron pan, but these kabobs will do well on a medium-hot grill. Start with the grill covered, then uncover for the last few minutes.

Serves 6

2 pork tenderloins, about 2 to 2½ pounds total, cut into 2-inch chunks

24 plump pitted prunes

2 medium onions, cut into quarters, layers separated

¼ cup extra-virgin olive oil

1½ teaspoons kosher salt

18 fresh bay leaves

Twelve 8-inch wooden or metal skewers, soaked in water for 15 minutes if wooden

In a large bowl, toss the pork, prunes, onions, and olive oil together. Season with salt. Thread the chunks of pork, prunes, onions, and bay leaves onto the skewers, alternating items.

Heat a large cast-iron pan or griddle (with cover) over medium heat. Sear the kabobs to brown the pork on all sides, about 5 minutes in all. Cover the pan, and reduce the heat to medium. Cook until the pork is cooked through but still juicy, about 15 minutes. Uncover, and let the pan juices reduce for a few minutes, turning the kabobs occasionally to glaze them with the juices. Serve immediately.

PORK MEDALLIONS WITH GRAPES AND PEARL ONIONS

Medaglioni di Maiale con Uva e Cipolline

You can get grapes year-round, but, as you know by now, I love cooking in season, so for this recipe I would change the fruit with the season. Peaches would be great in early summer, as would fresh figs in late summer. Apples and pears would be delightful in the winter. The one thing you need to calibrate is the time it takes for the fruits to cook. So add the fruit earlier if you're using apples or pears, or later if peaches or figs.

Serves 6

1 teaspoon kosher salt, plus more for the pot

12 cipolline onions (about 12 ounces), peeled

2 pork tenderloins, about 2 pounds total

4 tablespoons unsalted butter

2 tablespoons extra-virgin olive oil

All-purpose flour, for dredging

½ cup dry white wine

6 fresh sage leaves

1 tablespoon balsamic vinegar

8 ounces seedless green grapes, removed from stems (about 2 cups)

Bring a medium pot of salted water to boil, add the onions, and cook until almost tender but not falling apart, about 8 to 10 minutes. Drain and set aside, reserving 1 cup of the onion-cooking water.

Cut each pork tenderloin into six chunks. With a meat mallet, pound each to a thickness of about ½ inch.

In a large skillet, over medium heat, melt 2 tablespoons of the butter in the olive oil. Spread flour on a plate for dredging. Season the pork with ½ teaspoon of salt, and lightly dredge it in the flour. Brown the pork on both sides, about 2 minutes per side, and remove to a plate.

Add the onions to the skillet, and let them cook a few minutes, until lightly caramelized. Add the white wine, and bring to a boil. Once the wine is almost reduced, add the sage, the reserved onion-cooking water, and the remaining ½ teaspoon of salt. Let the sauce simmer for a few minutes, until it is reduced by almost half. Whisk in the vinegar and the remaining 2 tablespoons of butter. Add the pork back to the skillet with the grapes, and simmer until sauce is thickened and grapes just begin to soften, about 3 to 4 minutes.

HAM IN MARSALA SAUCE

Prosciutto Cotto al Marsala

Cured ham or prosciutto is very common in Italy, whereas cooked ham, known as prosciutto cotto, *is less so, and usually used for sandwiches and antipasti. But here is a version that includes the Italian Marsala flavor and treats the ham slice like a* scaloppina, *with very delicious results. When your family is craving baked ham but you do not have the time, here is a flavorful alternative.*

Serves 6

2 tablespoons unsalted butter

¼ cup extra-virgin olive oil

2 bone-in ham steaks, about
    2½ pounds total

2 leeks, white and light-green parts
    only, chopped (about 2 cups)

2 tablespoons all-purpose flour

1 cup dry Marsala

Kosher salt, to taste

In a large skillet, melt the butter in 2 tablespoons of olive oil over medium-high heat. Brown the ham steaks on both sides, and remove to a plate.

Once the ham steaks are out of the skillet, add the leeks, and cook until softened, about 3 to 4 minutes.

Add the remaining 2 tablespoons of olive oil and the flour. Cook and stir to make a roux. Cook until the roux smells toasted but is not colored, about a minute or two. Add the Marsala wine and ½ cup of water, and bring to a simmer. Nestle the ham steaks in the sauce, and simmer to blend the flavors, about 5 minutes. Taste the sauce, and add salt if necessary.

PORK POCKETS STUFFED WITH PICKLES AND CHEESE

Portafogli di Maiale

You could use the more expensive veal cutlets in this easy recipe, but I find pork cutlets wonderful and very tender when cooked in this fashion. This is a practical dish if you have company, too: once you have pan-fried it, it is finished in the oven. What is great about this dish is that it keeps well in the oven after it is done for 15 minutes without overcooking. Just shut off the oven, and cover the pan with aluminum foil until you are ready to serve.

Serves 6

6 boneless pork chops, about 7 to 8 ounces each

4 ounces shredded Italian Fontina

3 ounces deli ham, chopped

6 cornichons, chopped

2 plum tomatoes, seeded and chopped (about 1 cup)

1¼ teaspoons kosher salt

2 tablespoons unsalted butter

2 tablespoons extra-virgin olive oil

All-purpose flour, for dredging

¼ cup white wine

Juice of 1 lemon

2 tablespoons chopped fresh Italian parsley

Preheat the oven to 400 degrees F. Press each pork chop with one hand. With a sharp knife, cut a pocket in the meat of each pork chop, from side to side going deep into the meat, then pound each flap to about ¾-inch thickness. In a medium bowl, combine the Fontina, ham, cornichons, and tomatoes. Divide the stuffing, stuff the pocket of each chop, and secure with toothpicks. Season the outside of the meat with ½ teaspoon of salt.

Heat a large skillet over medium heat. Melt the butter in the olive oil. When the butter is melted, lightly dredge the pork in flour, and add them to the skillet. Brown on both sides, about 3 minutes per side. Add the wine, lemon juice, and remaining ¾ teaspoon of salt. Bring the sauce to a boil, then transfer the skillet to the oven, and bake, uncovered, until they are cooked through and the cheese is melted, about 15 minutes. (For a more polished-looking finished dish, you may want to strain the sauce before serving, if there are pieces of filling and melted cheese floating around in it, but this isn't necessary.) Stir in the parsley (whether you've strained or not) and serve.

PORK AND BEANS

Fagioli con Carne di Maiale

People shy away from dried legumes, but they are economical, nutritionally sensible, and rich in flavor. The only requirement is that they soak overnight for proper cooking. After that, it is smooth sailing.

Serves 6

1 pound dry cannellini, soaked overnight

2 meaty ham hocks, halved (ask your butcher to do this for you)

1 medium onion, chopped

2 large carrots, peeled and chopped

3 celery stalks, chopped

4 fresh bay leaves or 6 dried

2 fresh rosemary sprigs, needles stripped

¼ cup extra-virgin olive oil

2 teaspoons kosher salt

Drain and rinse the beans.

Put the ham hocks in a pot with water to cover, bring to a boil, and simmer 10 minutes, to remove some of the saltiness. Drain and rinse.

In a large pot, combine the blanched ham hocks, onion, carrots, celery, bay leaves, rosemary, and 2 quarts of water. Bring to a simmer, simmer for 15 minutes to blend the flavors, and then add the beans. Cover, and cook until the beans are tender, about 1 hour, adding a little more water as necessary to keep the beans soupy.

To finish, stir in the oil and salt, and let the mixture steep about 15 minutes, off heat, before serving.

DESSERTS

Some Tasty and Easy "Dulcis in Fundo"

Even though Italy has one of the largest repertoires of dessert recipes, dessert is not big on Italian tables after a good meal. Fresh fruits baked in a crust, cool granitas, and cookies, on the other hand, do make their appearance, and are lingered over while drinking an espresso.

Pastries are served a lot for breakfast, with coffee, or in the afternoon, as desserts with a cappuccino, and they are not always made with the double-zero white flour traditionally used in baking; cornmeal (Corn and Walnut Cake, page 242), almond flour (Caprese Torte, page 243), oats (Pear Crumble, page 248, and Oatmeal Crêpes, page 253), semolina (Anise Cookies, page 258), and chestnut flour are commonly used. I encourage you as well to mix and substitute some of these flours in recipes that you use and like. Such freedom to experiment will give you great results and satisfaction.

I particularly enjoy dessert recipes made with "savory" ingredients, which the Italians do best—rice (Rice Pudding with a Blessing, page 250 and Rice Zuccotto, page 251), squash (Yellow Squash Pie, page 244), or recycled bread (Pear Bread Pudding, page 247).

I love using fresh herbs in desserts (sage to infuse panna cotta, rosemary to make olive oil pound cake) and when mint overflows in my garden I turn it into into a refreshing easy-to-make granita. I also add the mint as the aromatic when making a granita with overripe seasonal peaches. All kinds of ripe fruit pulp will become granita, coarse crystals of ice within a few hours in your freezer. Granita can be made in advance, or even the day before; if you find that it has solidified too much, just drop it into the blender and make a great slush, to which you can add some Prosecco or vodka. That will turn it all into a great, feisty ending to a meal or to be enjoyed as a refreshing aperitif.

ANGEL CAKE

Torta dell'Angelo

This is a simple and light dessert that you will make over and over again in many different ways. It is great by itself, with some chocolate or fruit syrup poured over it, or topped with ice cream and berries. In the winter, I like it with poached or baked winter fruits, such as pears, apples, or quince.

Serves 8

1 cup cake flour

1½ cups confectioners' sugar, plus more for dusting the cake

Pinch kosher salt

12 large egg whites, at room temperature

1 teaspoon cream of tartar

1 cup granulated sugar

2 teaspoons vanilla extract

Zest of 1 lemon, grated

Fresh berries, for serving

Preheat the oven to 350 degrees F. Sift together the flour, confectioners' sugar, and salt onto a piece of parchment paper.

In a mixer fitted with the whisk attachment, beat the egg whites and cream of tartar until foamy. While beating on medium-high, gradually add in the granulated sugar, and beat until stiff peaks form, about 5 minutes. Add the vanilla and lemon zest, and mix in.

Remove the bowl from the mixer, and fold in about a third of the flour mixture. Gently fold in the remaining flour in two more additions.

Scrape the batter into a 10-inch ungreased tube pan. Do not grease the angel food baking pan; since this is basically a meringue cake, it needs to climb the sides of the pan while baking. This will not happen properly if the pan is greased. Bake until the top is lightly golden and a toothpick inserted in the center comes out clean, about 45 minutes.

Cool upside down on the counter (if your pan has "legs"), or invert and cool on the neck of a glass bottle. Let cool completely. Run the edges of a knife around the pan to loosen and unmold. Cut into wedges with a serrated knife, and serve with a dusting of confectioners' sugar and fresh berries.

ALMOND AND COFFEE CREAM MINI-TARTS

Tartellette alla Crema di Mandorle e Caffè

These mini-tarts are delightful as a finger-food dessert, and although here they are coffee-almond-flavored, you can change the flavoring according to your liking or what you have. A simple egg custard with some jam at the bottom of these tarts can be a great option.

Serves 8

DOUGH

2 cups all-purpose flour

3 tablespoons sugar

¼ teaspoon kosher salt

12 tablespoons unsalted cold butter, cut into pieces (1½ sticks)

3 egg yolks

2 tablespoons ice water, plus more as needed

COFFEE CREAM

1½ cups milk

1 tablespoon instant espresso powder

3 large egg yolks

6 tablespoons sugar

Pinch kosher salt

2 tablespoons cornstarch

1 tablespoon all-purpose flour

½ teaspoon almond extract

½ cup heavy cream, whipped to soft peaks

¼ cup sliced almonds, toasted, for serving

For the dough: In a food processor, pulse together the flour, sugar, and salt. Drop in the butter, and pulse until the mixture looks like coarse crumbs. Beat together the egg yolks and water, and pour into the processor. Pulse until the dough just comes together, adding a little water if crumbly, or a little flour if it is too wet. On the counter, knead the dough a few times; then flatten it into a disk, wrap in plastic, and chill for at least 30 minutes.

Preheat the oven to 400 degrees F. Roll out the dough on a floured surface to about ⅛-inch thick. Cut out eight rounds to fit into eight individual 4½-inch fluted mini-tart pans. Fit the dough into the pans, and trim so the dough is flush with the rims. Chill for 15 minutes, then place on a sheet pan. Dock the dough with a fork, and place parchment circles filled with pie weights or beans in each tart.

Bake until the dough is set but still blond in color, about 10 minutes. Remove the parchment and the weights, and continue baking until the dough is crisp and golden, about 10 to 15 minutes more. Remove from the oven, and cool on racks.

For the coffee cream: In a saucepan, bring the milk just to a simmer, and whisk in the espresso powder. In a medium bowl, whisk together the egg yolks, sugar, salt, cornstarch, and flour until smooth. Whisk in the hot milk a little at a time, tempering the eggs. Pour the mixture back into the saucepan over low heat until it just begins to simmer and thickens. Strain it into a clean bowl, stir in the almond extract, and chill, covering the surface with plastic wrap to keep it from forming a skin.

When the cream is chilled, fold in the whipped cream. Dollop the coffee cream into cooled tart shells, and garnish with almonds. Serve.

CORN AND WALNUT CAKE

Torta di Grano e Noci

I recall this simple cake from my childhood; it is the Italian version of pound cake, a bit lighter and with a granular texture. It is wonderful served for dessert with some ice cream and berries, or just toasted for breakfast. It keeps for a week or more.

Serves 6 to 8

¼ cup golden raisins

¼ cup brandy

1 stick unsalted butter, at room temperature, plus more for the pan

¾ cup sugar

4 large eggs, at room temperature

Zest of 1 lemon, grated

1 teaspoon vanilla extract

1 cup all-purpose flour, plus more for the pan

½ cup fine cornmeal

¼ cup cornstarch

1 teaspoon baking powder

¼ teaspoon kosher salt

Preheat the oven to 350 degrees F. Butter and flour a 9-inch springform pan. Soak the raisins in the brandy to plump them.

In a mixer fitted with the paddle attachment, cream the butter and sugar on high speed until light and fluffy. Add the eggs one at a time, beating well between the additions. Once all the eggs are added, beat on high speed for a minute to lighten the batter. Beat in the lemon zest and vanilla.

In a bowl, whisk together the flour, cornmeal, cornstarch, baking powder, and salt. Add to the mixer, and mix on low speed just to combine. Drain the raisins, and add them to the batter, mixing again just to distribute them. Spread the batter into the prepared pan, and bake on the middle rack of the oven until a toothpick inserted in the center comes out clean, about 30 minutes. Cool the cake on a rack before unmolding.

CAPRESE TORTE

Torta Caprese

This is a great moist chocolate-flavored dessert. It's easy to make, and it keeps well for several days.

Serves 8

1¼ cups blanched sliced almonds, toasted

1 stick unsalted butter, plus more for the pan

8 ounces bittersweet chocolate, chopped

2 tablespoons dried breadcrumbs

4 large eggs, at room temperature, separated

1 cup sugar

Zest of 1 orange, grated

2 tablespoons amaro or rum

¼ teaspoon kosher salt

Confectioners' sugar, for garnish

Preheat the oven to 350 degrees F. In a food processor, grind the almonds until fine but not powdery. Melt the stick of butter in a double boiler with the chocolate, stirring to combine, then let cool slightly.

Grease a 9-inch springform pan with butter, and sprinkle with the breadcrumbs. Tap around to coat the bottom and sides of the pan with the breadcrumbs, and tap out any excess.

In a mixer fitted with the paddle attachment, on medium-high speed, whisk the egg yolks and ¾ cup of the sugar until thick and pale golden in color, about 2 minutes. Beat in the orange zest, the amaro or rum, and the salt. On low speed, beat in the cooled chocolate mixture just until smooth. Fold in the ground almonds.

In the mixer, in a clean bowl fitted with the whisk attachment, whisk the egg whites and remaining ¼ cup sugar to stiff peaks. Stir a third of the whites into the chocolate mixture, then gently fold in the rest. Spread into the prepared springform pan, and bake until the top is firm and crackly (a toothpick will still come out with some thick batter on it), about 35 to 40 minutes.

Let the cake cool on a rack for 5 minutes, then run a knife around the edge to loosen it, and unmold. Serve sprinkled with confectioners' sugar.

YELLOW SQUASH PIE

Torta di Zucca Gialla

The idea for this recipe came to me from The Art of Eating Well. *This is my interpretation of the recipe from Pellegrino Artusi's* La scienza in cucina e l'arte di mangiar bene, *the first truly successful Italian cookbook. I love cooking with squash, especially in the fall, when it is in season. One would normally think of this as a savory dish, but it makes a delicious dessert.*

Serves 6 to 8

2 pounds yellow squash, grated

2 cups whole milk

½ cup sugar

¼ teaspoon kosher salt

1 tablespoon unsalted butter, at room temperature

½ cup panko breadcrumbs

¼ teaspoon ground cinnamon

4 ounces blanched almonds

3 eggs

Preheat oven to 350 degrees F. Wrap grated squash in a kitchen towel, and wring out any excess liquid. Put squash in a medium saucepan with the milk, 2 tablespoons sugar, and the salt. Simmer until squash is tender, about 15 minutes. Let cool slightly.

Butter an 8- or 9-inch glass pie plate. In a small bowl, toss together the panko and cinnamon. Line the pie plate with the panko, tapping out and discarding the excess.

In a food processor, grind the almonds into fine crumbs with the remaining 6 tablespoons sugar. Add the cooled squash and the eggs. Purée until smooth. Pour into the lined baking dish, and bake until set, about 45 minutes. Let cool slightly on a rack before cutting into wedges. Can be served warm or at room temperature.

GRANDMA ROSA'S APPLE CAKE

Torta di Mele di Nonna Rosa

Moist and delicious, this is a fruit dessert that you can make year-round. I especially love making it in the fall, when apples are in season. It is also perfect for breakfast. When you have a big crowd coming, pop one of these into the oven, and your guests will devour it along with a dollop of whipped cream and a good cup of coffee.

Serves 8

1 stick unsalted butter, at room temperature, plus more for the pan

1 cup all-purpose flour, plus more for the pan

¾ cup granulated white sugar

2 large eggs

½ teaspoon vanilla extract

1 tablespoon baking powder

Pinch kosher salt

Zest of 1 lemon, grated

3 baking apples (such as Golden Delicious), peeled, cored, and cut into ½-inch chunks

2 tablespoons light-brown sugar

½ cup coarsely chopped walnuts, toasted

Preheat the oven to 350 degrees F. Butter and flour an 8- or 9-inch springform pan.

In an electric mixer fitted with the paddle attachment, cream the butter and white sugar until pale and light, about 1 minute. Add the eggs, one at a time, and beat until light and fluffy, another minute or two. Beat in the vanilla.

Sift together the flour, baking powder, and salt. Pour the dry ingredients into the mixer with the lemon zest, and mix until just combined. In a medium bowl, toss together the apples, brown sugar, and walnuts. Scrape the batter into the prepared pan, smooth the top, and then sprinkle with the apple mixture.

Bake until a toothpick comes out clean from the center of the cake, about 35 to 40 minutes. Let cool on a rack, then unmold, and cut into wedges to serve.

PEAR BREAD PUDDING

Budino di Pere e Pane

You know how much I love to recycle food and not waste anything. Well, bread pudding is a delicious and comforting dessert that does just that. It is easy to make, and easy to serve: just top it with a dollop of whipped cream and it is good every time.

This recipe has pears and almonds added to it, which gives it that fruity pear taste and almond crunch. The nuts can be changed according to preference, as can the fruit according to season.

Serves 6 to 8

2 tablespoons softened unsalted butter

6 large eggs

1 cup sugar

1 teaspoon vanilla extract

Zest of 1 lemon, grated

1 cup milk

1 cup heavy cream, plus more to whip for garnish

4 cups day-old ½-inch country-bread cubes, crusts removed

2 Bosc pears, peeled, cored, and cut into ½-inch chunks

⅓ cup blanched sliced almonds

Preheat the oven to 350 degrees F. Coat the baking dish with softened butter. Whisk the eggs in a large bowl. Add all but 2 tablespoons of the sugar, the vanilla, and lemon zest, and whisk to lighten the mixture. Whisk in the milk and heavy cream. Add the bread and pears, and pour the mixture into the prepared baking dish.

Sprinkle with the remaining 2 tablespoons of sugar and the almond slices. Bake until the pudding is set and puffy and the top is golden, about 40 to 45 minutes. Let cool on a rack for 15 minutes; serve warm or at room temperature, garnished with whipped cream.

PEAR CRUMBLE

Crumble di Pere

This version of a crumble has a hearty fall-and-winter feel, but it can be made with any other seasonal fruits as well. The dried cherries give great flavor and texture to the filling, while the oats give a nutty crunch to the crumble.

Serves 6

6 tablespoons cold unsalted butter, cut into bits, plus more for the baking dish

1 cup dried cherries

¼ cup brandy

6 firm Bosc pears, peeled, cored, and cut into 1-inch chunks

¾ cup granulated white sugar

Grated zest and juice of 1 lemon

½ cup old-fashioned oats

½ cup all-purpose flour

½ packed cup light-brown sugar

¼ cup chopped blanched almonds

Pinch kosher salt

Unsweetened whipped cream, for serving

Preheat the oven to 375 degrees F. Butter a 3-quart baking dish (a flat oval dish gives the best topping-to-fruit ratio). Combine the cherries and brandy, and let macerate for 15 to 20 minutes.

In a large bowl, combine the soaked cherries, pears, white sugar, lemon zest, and juice. Spread in the baking dish.

In a food processor, combine the oats, flour, brown sugar, almonds, and salt. Pulse to combine, then drop in the butter pieces. Pulse until the mixture forms clumps the size of peas. Sprinkle over the fruit, and don't pack it down.

Bake until browned and bubbly, about 45 minutes. Let cool on a rack for 15 minutes before serving warm with whipped cream.

RICE PUDDING WITH A BLESSING
Riso delle Monache

In Italy, we owe a lot to convents and monasteries for preserving culinary and beverage customs. Here is a recipe as the nuns in the convent made it. Rice pudding is a favorite comfort food. In this recipe, apples are added to the cooked rice, then all is baked. My mouth waters just thinking about it.

Serves 6 to 8

1 cup Arborio rice

2½ cups whole milk

½ teaspoon kosher salt

1 cup granulated white sugar

2 tablespoons unsalted butter

6 Golden Delicious or other baking apples, peeled, cored, and sliced ¼ inch thick

1 cup raisins

Grated zest and juice of 1 lemon

2 large eggs

¼ lightly packed cup brown sugar

Preheat the oven to 375 degrees F. In a medium saucepan, combine the rice, 2 cups of the milk, the salt, and ½ cup of the sugar. Simmer until all of the milk is absorbed and the rice is al dente, about 13 minutes. Stir in the butter until melted. Let cool slightly.

In another medium saucepan, over medium heat, combine the apples, raisins, lemon zest and juice, and remaining ½ cup of sugar. Stir until the sugar is melted, then simmer until the apples release their juices and just begin to soften, about 5 minutes. Let cool slightly.

In a large bowl, combine the rice and apple mixtures. Whisk together the remaining ½ cup of milk and the eggs. Pour this over the rice and apples, and mix well. Spread in a 2-to-3-quart baking dish, and bake for 15 minutes. Then sprinkle with the brown sugar, and continue baking until it's set and the top is caramelized, about 15 minutes more. Let cool slightly, but serve warm.

RICE ZUCCOTTO

Zuccotto di Riso

A zuccotto *is the little round cap that cardinals wear, and this dessert gets its name and shape from that cap. Most* zuccotti *are made with a creamy filling that is put into a bowl lined with* pasta genovese *(or pound cake); it is covered, chilled well, then inverted out and decorated, usually with confectioners' sugar. Here, instead, we have a combination of rice and* crema pasticcera, *or pastry cream, a different and quite delicious filling. The* zuccotto *recipe is easy, and the results are impressive.*

Serves 8

1 cup Arborio rice

2 cups milk

14 tablespoons granulated sugar (¾ cup plus 2 tablespoons)

Pinch kosher salt

4 ounces diced candied citron

Juice of 2 lemons

Zest of 1 lemon, grated

1 cup heavy cream

2 small (11½ ounces each) pound cakes, sliced ½ inch thick

Confectioners' sugar, for garnish (optional)

In a medium saucepan, combine the rice, milk, ¼ cup sugar, and pinch of salt. Bring to a simmer, and cook gently until the rice absorbs the milk, about 15 minutes. About halfway through the cooking time, stir in the candied citron. Scrape the rice onto a sheet pan to cool, then chill completely in the refrigerator.

While the rice chills, make the lemon syrup. In a small saucepan, combine the lemon juice and zest with 1 cup of water and ½ cup of sugar. Bring to a boil, and cook until reduced by about half. Let cool to room temperature.

Whisk the heavy cream to soft peaks, adding the remaining 2 tablespoons of sugar toward the end. Fold the cream gently into the chilled rice.

To assemble: Line a 3-quart bowl with plastic wrap, with a few inches overhanging all around. Line the bowl with slices of pound cake, pressing to adhere, and cutting the slices to make a tight fight as necessary. Brush generously with some of the syrup. Scoop the rice filling into the lined bowl, and spread in an even layer with a spatula. Top with remaining pound-cake slices, covering the filling completely, cutting to fit as necessary. Brush with remaining syrup. Cover the bowl tightly with plastic wrap, and chill overnight in the refrigerator.

To serve: Uncover and unmold onto a serving plate. Carefully peel off plastic wrap, and dust *zuccotto* with confectioners' sugar. Cut into wedges and serve.

OATMEAL CRÊPES

Palacinke di Avena

In Croatia, crêpes are called palacinke; *they are called* omlet *in Trieste, a city in the north-eastern region of Italy, Friuli–Venezia Giulia, the area I come from. Every culture has some form of crêpes. My family, especially the grandchildren, love them. I always ate them as a child and I still make them regularly. In this recipe, instead of making them entirely of white flour, I incorporate some oatmeal. It makes nutritional sense and the oats add a nutty flavor and texture to the crêpes.*

Makes 12 to 14

2 large eggs

½ teaspoon vanilla extract

Grated zest of 1 lemon

1½ cups oat flour (or grind oatmeal in a food processor or blender)

1 cup all-purpose flour

3 tablespoons granulated sugar

4 tablespoons unsalted butter, melted and cooled

Olive oil, for cooking the crêpes

1 cup jam of your choice, for filling the crêpes

Confectioners' sugar or whipped cream and sliced toasted almonds, for serving

In a large bowl, whisk together the eggs, 3 cups of water, vanilla, and lemon zest. Whisk in the oat flour, all-purpose flour, and sugar until smooth, but don't overmix. Whisk in the butter.

Place a 10-inch nonstick skillet over medium-high heat, and brush the skillet with olive oil. When the oil is hot, pour in ⅓ cup batter, and quickly turn the skillet in a circle with your wrist to coat the entire bottom of the skillet evenly with the batter. Cook until brown on one side, about 30 seconds to a minute. With a spatula, flip the crêpe, and brown the other side, another 15 to 30 seconds. Remove to a plate, and repeat with remaining crêpe batter.

To serve, fill the warm crêpes with about a tablespoon of jam each. Fold over into quarters, like a handkerchief, and dust with confectioners' sugar, or roll them into a tube. For a fancier presentation top with some whipped cream and toasted sliced almonds.

ORANGES IN MARSALA

Arance al Marsala

Sicily produces the best oranges in the world, bar none, as well as the delicious sweet wine Marsala, a wine created in the late eighteenth century by J. Woodhouse, an English merchant who wanted to import it from Sicily to England. So that the wine would survive the long hot trip, he fortified the local Marsala, like sherry or port. His first shipment reached England in 1783 and was a huge success. Marsala is 16 to 17 percent alcohol, and can be either dry or sweet. In this case, I'd go with the sweeter one.

Serves 4 to 6

6 navel oranges

½ cup sugar

1 cup Marsala wine

Fresh mint sprigs, for garnish

With a paring knife, cut the peel from the oranges, removing the white pith as well. Cut the oranges crosswise into ½-inch slices.

Layer a third of the orange slices in a glass serving bowl. Sprinkle with half of the sugar and a third of the Marsala wine. Layer another third of the oranges, then the remaining sugar, and another third of the Marsala. Top with the remaining oranges, and pour over them the remaining Marsala.

Cover, and refrigerate until well chilled, at least 2 hours. Serve garnished with mint.

FRIED HALF-MOONS

Mezzelune Fritte

I love simple butter dough stuffed or topped with jam. Most of the desserts of my childhood were based on fruit—fresh, dried, or preserved. Fruit carried the flavor. Here the jam is stuffed into the dough and fried, but to save a few calories you can bake these delicious morsels instead, and they will be just as good.

Makes about 24

3 cups all-purpose flour, plus more
    for rolling

1 tablespoon granulated sugar

¼ teaspoon kosher salt

12 tablespoons (1½ sticks) cold
    butter, cut into pieces

⅓ cup ice water, plus more if needed

1 large egg yolk

1½ cups thick, chunky preserves,
    such as apricot or cherry

Vegetable oil, for frying

Confectioners' sugar, for dusting

In a food processor, combine flour, granulated sugar, and salt, and pulse to combine. Drop in the butter pieces, and pulse until the mixture resembles coarse crumbs. In a measuring cup, mix together the water and egg yolk. Drizzle over the flour, and pulse just until the dough comes together in a ball; add a little more flour or water to adjust the consistency as necessary. Dump the dough onto a floured counter, and knead once or twice to form a disk. Wrap in plastic, and let it rest in the refrigerator for 30 minutes.

Roll the dough on a floured surface to about ⅛ inch thick. With a floured 2½-inch cutter, cut into rounds; transfer them to parchment-lined baking sheets. Reroll scraps, and roll out once more, until you get about twenty-four rounds.

Fill each round with a scant tablespoon of preserves. Sealing the edges with water, fold over to make a half-moon. Crimp closed with a fork. Chill in refrigerator while the oil heats.

Heat several inches of vegetable oil in a deep pot to 365 degrees F. Fry, in batches, until golden brown on both sides, about 5 to 6 minutes per batch. Drain on paper towels. To serve, dust lightly with confectioners' sugar.

Facing page, left to right: Fried Half-Moons, Mint Granita (page 260), Peach Granita (page 259)

ANISE COOKIES

Biscotti all'Anice

Anise is a favorite Italian flavoring, especially for cookies. Serve these with espresso coffee and some anisette liqueur, and you will take your guests to Italy.

Makes about 48

COOKIES

1¾ cups all-purpose flour

1 cup fine semolina

1 teaspoon baking powder

½ teaspoon baking soda

¼ teaspoon kosher salt

1 large egg plus 2 egg yolks

2 tablespoons sambuca

½ teaspoon anise extract

12 tablespoons (1½ sticks) unsalted butter, at room temperature

1 cup granulated sugar

GLAZE

2 tablespoons milk

¼ teaspoon anise extract

1 cup confectioners' sugar, sifted

In a bowl, stir together flour, semolina, baking powder, baking soda, and salt. In a spouted measuring cup, whisk together the egg, yolks, sambuca, and anise extract. In a mixer fitted with the paddle attachment, cream the butter and sugar until the combination is light and fluffy, about 2 minutes.

Add the egg-yolk mixture to the mixer, and beat on medium until smooth. Add the flour mixture, and beat on low just until combined. Remove dough from mixing bowl, wrap it with plastic, and chill it until firm, about 1 hour.

Preheat the oven to 350 degrees F. Roll the dough into four dozen balls, and bake in batches on parchment-lined sheet pans, rotating the pans from the top to bottom racks in your oven halfway through the baking time, until golden, about 16 to 18 minutes per batch. Cool completely on racks.

For the glaze: Whisk the milk and anise extract into the confectioners' sugar to make a smooth glaze about the thickness of pancake batter. Add a little more milk or confectioners' sugar to adjust the consistency. Dip or drizzle the cookies with glaze, and let set on a rack.

PEACH GRANITA

Sorbetto di Pesce

Granita can be made of any deliciously ripe fruit; here the combination of aromatic peaches and Prosecco make for a festive delight.

Serves 4

1 cup Prosecco

1 cup sugar

Juice of 2 lemons

6 fresh mint sprigs

Pinch kosher salt

5 ripe medium-sized peaches (about 2 pounds), chopped

In a small saucepan, combine the Prosecco, sugar, juice of one lemon, mint, and salt. Bring to a simmer, and cook just to melt the sugar, about 2 minutes. Remove from heat, and let cool.

When the Prosecco syrup has cooled, put it in a blender with the peaches and remaining lemon juice. Purée until smooth.

Pour into a wide, shallow metal pan so the mixture comes about an inch up the sides. Put in the freezer. Once ice crystals begin to form around the sides of the pan, after about an hour, scrape the granita with a fork to incorporate the crystals back into the slush. Keep freezing and scraping every ½ hour to an hour, until the granita is completely frozen in light, fluffy crystals, around 6 hours.

MINT GRANITA

Granita alla Menta

Granita, the Italian version of sorbet, granular in texture, is easy to make and quite refreshing after a good meal. Italians prefer fruit or a granita after a meal, rather than a complex dessert.

Serves 6

1¾ cups sugar

1 large bunch mint, washed (about 2 packed cups)

Juice of 2 lemons

2 mint herbal tea bags (not black tea)

Put the sugar in a medium saucepan with 2 cups of water, and bring to a simmer. Simmer until the sugar is completely dissolved. Stir in the mint and lemon juice. Remove from the heat, add the tea bags, and steep for 15 minutes. Strain and cool.

Pour into a wide, shallow metal pan so the granita comes about an inch up the sides. Put in the freezer. Once ice crystals begin to form around the sides of the pan, after about an hour, scrape the granita with a fork to incorporate the crystals back into the slush. Keep freezing and scraping every ½ hour to an hour, until the granita is completely frozen in light, fluffy crystals, about 6 hours.

Index

(Page references in *italic* refer to illustrations.)

A Note About the Authors

Lidia Matticchio Bastianich was born in Pula, Istria, and came to the United States in 1958. She opened her first restaurant, Buonavia, in Queens in 1971 with her husband, Feice, and a second restaurant, Villa Secondo, shortly thereafter. Their tremendous success inspired them to launch Felidia in 1981 in Manhattan, followed by Becco, Esca, Del Posto, and Eataly (also in New York), and Lidia's in Kansas City and Pittsburgh. She has developed a line of Lidia's Pasta and Lidia's Sauces, available across the United States.

Lidia Bastianich is the author of ten previous books, *La Cucina di Lidia, Lidia's Italian Table, Lidia's Italian-American Kitchen, Lidia's Family Table, Lidia's Italy, Lidia Cooks from the Heart of Italy, Lidia's Italy in America, Lidia's Favorite Recipes* (the last four with Tanya Bastianich Manuali), and her two children's books, *Nonna Tell Me a Story* and *Lidia's Family Kitchen: Nonna's Birthday Surprise*. She has also been the host of several public television series—*Lidia's Italian Table, Lidia's Italian-American Kitchen, Lidia's Family Table, Lidia's Italy, Lidia's Italy in America,* and *Lidia Celebrates America*—and she gives lectures on Italian cuisine across the country. Lidia also has developed a very interactive website, www.lidiasitaly.com, where she shares daily recipes, pictures, information about seasonal products, tips, and personal stories. She lives on Long Island.

Tanya Bastianich Manuali's visits to Italy as a child sparked her passion for the country's art and culture. She dedicated herself to the study of Italian Renaissance art during her college years at Georgetown, and earned a master's degree from Syracuse University and a doctorate from Oxford University. Living and studying in many regions of Italy for seven years, she taught art history to American students in Florence, and also met her husband, Corrado Manuali, from Rome. Tanya created Esperienze Italiane, a custom-tour company devoted to the discovery of Italian food, wine, and art. Tanya is integrally involved in the production of Lidia's public television series and is active daily in the family restaurant business. She has also led the development of the website, lidiasitaly.com, and related publications and merchandise lines of tabletop and cookware. Together with her husband, Corrado, Tanya oversees the production and expansion of Lidia's food line, which includes ten cuts of pasta, seven sauces, and fresh meals for nationwide distribution. Tanya has coauthored four previous books with her mother: *Lidia's Favorite Recipes, Lidia's Italy, Lidia Cooks from the Heart of Italy,* and *Lidia's Italy in America*. In 2010, Tanya coauthored *Reflections of the Breast: Breast Cancer in Art Through the Ages,* a social-art-historical look at breast cancer in art from ancient Egypt to today. Tanya and Corrado live in New York City with their children, Lorenzo and Julia.